Using Semi-Structured Interviews in Small-Scale Research

A TEACHER'S GUIDE

Eric Drever

The Scottish Council for Research in Education

SCRE Publication 129

Practitioner MiniPaper 15

First published 1995

Series editors: Wynne Harlen
                     Rosemary Wake

ISBN 1 86003 011 4

Printed and bound for the Scottish Council for Research in Education, 15 St John Street, Edinburgh EH8 8JR by GNP Booth, Glasgow.

Contents

Acknowledgements

Various people have contributed in some way to this work. The idea and broad outline of the book originated in discussions with Pamela Munn and Rosemary Wake. The material includes examples drawn from or stimulated by the various research projects funded by the Scottish Office Education Department and the work of students on the MEd programme in which I have been involved during my time at Stirling University, as researcher, tutor and above all as learner.

Special thanks are due to Rosemary Wake for her patience, and for editing the text in a way which managed to be at the same time meticulous and creative.

1

Why Use Interviews?

Interviewing is one of the commonest methods used in small-scale educational research. This is not surprising. In the teaching profession, when you want to get information, canvass opinion, or exchange ideas, the natural thing to do is to talk to people.

Besides, interviewing is a very flexible technique, suited to a wide range of research purposes. There are several styles or 'schools' of interviewing, each with rather different aims and based on different principles. At one extreme, the interviewer simply reads out a list of questions and alternative responses to the person being interviewed, who has to pick from the options offered. (You meet this approach if you are stopped by a market researcher in your local shopping centre.) At the other extreme the interviewer adopts a 'non-directive', almost conversational style, allowing the interviewee largely to determine the course of the discussion.

This book is about semi-structured interviews, which lie between these extremes. The name 'semi-structured' means that the interviewer sets up a general structure by deciding in advance what ground is to be covered and what main questions are to be asked. This leaves the detailed structure to be worked out during the interview. The person interviewed can answer at some length in his or her own words, and the interviewer responds using prompts, probes and follow-up questions to get the interviewee to clarify or expand on the answers.

Semi-structured interviews can yield a variety of kinds of information. Even within one interview you could:

- gather factual information about people's circumstances
- collect statements of their preferences and opinions
- explore in some depth their experiences, motivations and reasoning.

1

For example, in an evaluation of a resource-based teaching programme in chemistry, semi-structured interviews included questions to find out:

- the number of classes in each year group who were using the
  scheme and the range of ability in each class
- teachers' opinions on the quality of the teaching resources and
  assessment materials, and the quality of in-service support
- an account of how each school had learned about the course
  and decided to adopt it
- how teachers interpreted the main features of the programme,
  focusing on key terms used by the authors.

Some of these questions could have been asked in a postal questionnaire. These usually have a preponderance of fixed-response
'tick-the-box' items and a few questions requiring answers in the
respondent's own words. They have the advantage that they allow you to reach many more people for the same amount of effort,
although they do not give the same depth of information. Questionnaires too are a popular research technique and for many
teacher-researchers the decision about how to gather their data
boils down to a choice between questionnaires and interviews.
The next section aims to help you make that choice.

Interviews or questionnaires?

Like most decisions about research methods this one is not subject
to hard-and-fast rules. Two kinds of issues need to be considered.
Some are essentially practical: they arise from the limited time and
resources available to someone who is doing research on top of a
full-time job. Practical considerations are linked to more theoretical concerns, to do with the kind of research study you are at-
tempting, and the kind of understanding and explanation you can
hope to achieve. Some of the pros and cons are now considered.

Interviews give high-quality data

Most people if approached properly will agree to be interviewed.
You can expect them to treat the interview seriously and answer
all your questions. You can explain any ambiguities and correct

any misunderstandings of your questions, and if you are not sure about the answers you can probe for clarification. As a result you can expect to get a complete set of high quality data, from all your selected interviewees, and covering all your questions.

In some ways you can do even better than that. By going to interview someone you gain an impression of their home or workplace. During the interview you are aware of their manner, their body language. This may help you in conducting the interview or in interpreting it later. It is possible, too, that you will hit on a facet of your study that you had not anticipated in planning the interview. Even if it is too late to include it, you have learned something about the limitations of your research.

By comparison with interviews, questionnaires are inflexible once they are in print. This is especially the case with postal surveys. You have little control over them once they are in the mail. You may not get them back, and not have the time to chase them up individually. The answers may be incomplete, or there may be evidence that the questions have been misunderstood, or the whole thing treated frivolously. And you never learn anything you didn't ask!

Interviewing people takes time

A semi-structured interview usually takes about 45 minutes to an hour to complete. To this you may have to add time for travelling and some social chat, so that it becomes a case of one interview per morning or afternoon. If you are a teacher interviewing other teachers, you have to search for common free time, which may mean lunchtime or evenings. Even 20 interviews is a major undertaking, and each extra interview adds proportionately to the labour.

By contrast, a questionnaire study can readily encompass 100 people and still be 'small-scale', while covering 200 would not involve twice the work.

Processing interviews takes time

Once the interview is over, the work of processing remains. You may have to write up extensive notes that you made, hoping that you don't forget the significance of some of your more cryptic jottings. Or you may have to listen to an audio-tape, summarising some passages, writing out some answers in full, sometimes having to run the tape back to check on an earlier answer. All of this takes time. Then follows the analysis, in which you will find yourself reading the material over and over to make sense of the variety of answers resulting from the individual interviews.

With questionnaires the processing of results is more straightforward, to the point of being tedious. Mostly you are simply transferring data from a structured response sheet on to a similarly structured grid.

However, if the processing of interviews is hard work, it is also very interesting. You are constantly having to exercise judgement about how to summarise without distorting what people said or omitting anything important. The time and effort involved is not an argument against using interviews, but one for being modest in what you attempt and for thinking ahead. Above all you should not interview people 'on spec', or without having a clear idea how you will deal with the results.

Interviewing requires skill

An interview is not a conversation. It is a formal encounter, with a specific purpose, and both parties are aware of this. A common problem is that people are uneasy about maintaining formality especially with close colleagues, and they conclude that a 'naturalistic' style of interviewing is best: but 'naturalistic' interviewing is really a special case, with a distinctive purpose and theoretical basis, and requiring special skills.

Because teachers spend a lot of their time in the classroom asking questions, they are sometimes disconcerted to find that interviewing is different and quite difficult at first: difficult to take notes and maintain the flow, difficult to avoid leading questions, difficult to stick to a schedule. However, if they develop a well-prepared schedule, one that is not over-ambitious, then, with practice, most teachers quickly become competent at semi-structured interviewing.

Survey or case study?

A decision about whether to use interviews or questionnaires affects the kind of understanding you can hope to achieve from your research. One way of approaching this decision is to ask yourself whether you see your research mainly as a *survey*, or as a *case study*.

Surveys

A survey aims to provide a general picture of people's circumstances or opinions, across a 'population' that you have defined, for example:

- what kinds of resources do *modern studies teachers* use?
- what views do the parents have on the introduction of French in primary schools?
- what use do employers make of school examination results as a job entry qualification?

In a typical survey you select a sample from your population, and ask everyone the same questions in exactly the same way. Their replies to each question are coded, and from the patterns in this data, you can develop an account showing which responses are most common, what proportions of people express various views, and contrasting the replies of different groups within your sample. Using statistical checks you can then extrapolate these results with varying degrees of certainty to the general population of modern studies teachers, primary school parents, or employers.

The soundness of the findings depends critically on two factors: first, on having as large a sample as possible, and second, on controlling the questioning so as to get standardised information. Professional research organisations can carry out large scale surveys using teams of interviewers, working from detailed schedules. For the small-scale researcher this approach is neither feasible nor desirable. It ignores the great strength of the interview, which is its capacity to seek explanations by exploring individual view-points. And the number of people you can interview is too small for the results to show statistical significance.

If your aim is a large scale survey, then use a questionnaire, which is ideally suited to that purpose.

However, small scale surveys are also possible. In this the population is likely to be more limited and of local significance. You can use semi-structured interviews to gain greater depth of understanding than you could expect from a questionnaire.

For example you might look at:

- the changing roles of advisory personnel: a survey in one local authority area
- returning to education: experiences of students on a college 'Access' scheme
- teachers' interpretations of a new report form: a study in one school.

Here you are dealing with a smallish number of people in one region, college or school. You could aim to interview the whole of your population, avoiding any problems to do with sampling or the poor return of questionnaires. The main questions are the same for everyone, and are followed up in a standard way. The general aim is not to code and count the answers to each question separately, and draw conclusions from percentages and correlations, as you would with a large questionnaire study. Instead you would expect to use the flexibility of the interview and get people to explain their answers at length, and you draw on these statements to identify common features or distinctive views across the range of interviews.

The difference between the two approaches to surveys can be illustrated from two recent studies. The first was a questionnaire survey of about 400 teachers, investigating their views about opportunities for promotion. Amongst other patterns, their answers showed a highly significant correlation with age and years of experience, which suggested that after a time people assume they will progress no further up the career ladder. In the second study, 15 teachers were interviewed about their careers. Several of them referred to the way in which their expectations had changed during the time they had been in the profession. In both cases, the same age-related factor stood out. In the first case, it was extracted from the data by the researcher, and confidence in its importance was based on statistical significance; in the second it was 'in the data': said by the teachers in the interviews, and confidence in its importance stemmed from how that was expressed by the interviewees themselves.

Case studies

In a case study the researcher does not aim to cover a whole population and extract common factors, but to provide an in-depth picture of a particular area of the educational world, chosen because it is relatively self-contained (at least as far as the purposes of the research are concerned). The focus is often on a number of people who work together but have different roles, and the aim is to understand them as a group, with their different but interdependent functions and ways of thinking.

Topics for case studies might include:

- cross-subject collaboration in one school's health studies programme
- the effectiveness of a work-placement scheme run by one company
- the influence of its facilities on a PE department's curriculum planning
- individual students' experiences of curricular guidance and course continuity
- one school's provision for pupils with moderate learning difficulties
- one teacher's provision for pupils with moderate learning difficulties.

In each of these cases it should be easy to decide who is involved, and so should be included in the study. We could aim at quite detailed understanding of the factors at work in that particular case, without assuming that any other case would be the same. Another work-placement scheme, another school's provision, might be similar, but we would leave that possibility to be tested by others.

Semi-structured interviews are well-suited to such case studies. The researcher can adapt the main questions to suit people's complementary roles, and can explore their different perspectives in depth.

Interviews and questionnaires

Because interviews can provide depth of explanation within a particular context, while questionnaires paint a broad though possibly superficial picture, it is often a good idea to use both. An exploratory survey or case study using interviews may be used to identify the main issues to be built into a questionnaire, or a questionnaire survey may allow us to select interesting issues or cases to be followed up in depth through interviews.

Interviews and observation

At one time there was a fashion for classroom observation studies based on highly structured schedules. These tried to identify patterns of teacher activity representing successful practice. They were not very successful because they told only half the story. You saw what teachers did but you did not know the purpose and thinking that lay behind it. On the other hand, simply interviewing teachers about their teaching methods was not any better. Teachers tended to talk as much about general notions of good practice as about what actually happened in classrooms. However, by using classroom observation as the focus for a semi-structured interview soon after, researchers have gained rich information about how teachers think as well as about what they do.

Summary

Some points about interviewing, and semi-structured interviewing in particular. Semi-structured interviewing :

- is a very flexible technique, suitable for gathering information and opinions and exploring people's thinking and motivations
- yields rich information and guarantees good coverage
- takes time to do and analyse and so requires realistic planning
- cannot cover large numbers (use a questionnaire for that)
- requires a degree of skill (but that comes with practice)
- is useful in mini-surveys and case studies
- can be used along with other methods.

Something that is seldom mentioned is that interviewing is often an intensive and rewarding social experience! Often you will meet people years later, and they will remember, with pleasure, that you interviewed them (though they may not remember what it was about!).

2

Different Kinds of Interviews

Books on research methods classify interviews in a variety of ways: formal, less formal and informal; structured, semi-structured and unstructured; focused or non-directive; informant interviews versus respondent interviews. So how many really different types of interviews are there?

This chapter aims to dispel any confusion. It looks at the main characteristics of the semi-structured interview, concentrating on two key ideas: the structure of the interview, and how far the interviewer can exert control. Later it will draw a contrast briefly with the two other main types of interview.

Structure and control

Chapter 1 stressed that an interview is a formal encounter. People do not just decide to 'have an interview'. The interviewer initiates contact, the interviewee consents. Both parties know broadly what it is going to be about, and that it is 'on the record'. The result is not a conversation with people taking turns on an equal footing: the interviewer has established the right to ask questions, the interviewee has agreed to answer them. This gives the interviewer the initiative to structure the interview in advance by planning the main questions to be asked, and to control the interview as it happens by prompting, accepting or probing the answers.

A semi-structured interview

Let's look at how this works in a semi-structured interview. This example is taken from a study in which teachers using a new curriculum package were asked about the thinking behind it. The general aim is to encourage people to talk at some length and in their own way. Whether what they say is 'right' is not an issue. You may know that what they are describing is not how the authors intended their package to be used, but you carry on with your prompts and probes according to plan.

What the interviewer says is on the left of the page. The right hand side explains what is happening. Notice how the interviewer's main questions structure the discussion around 'key features' selected by the interviewer.

There are two main kinds of subordinate questions. Prompts are used to encourage interviewees to answer (PROMPT TYPE 1) and to ensure that they say as much as they can or wish to (PROMPT TYPE 2). Probes are used either to get the interviewee to expand in detail (PROBE TYPE 1), or explain further (PROBE TYPE 2).

Interview	*Commentary*
I: In this section I want to ask you about several of the key features that the authors consider important. I want to ask you what you think they intend, and about how this works in practice - OK?	Here the interviewer sets the scene, and checks that the interviewee understands what is coming. The response may be verbal or not - possibly just a nod.
I: They say it provides 'a multi-level scheme'. What do you think they mean by that?	This is the *first main question*, focusing on a phrase taken from the authors' rationale for the programme.
R: (no reply – respondent uncertain)	
I: Well, they say: 'Pupils find their own level and work with appropriate extension material'...	The interviewer supplies another phrase of the authors' to encourage the respondent to answer (PROMPT TYPE 1).
R: (respondent replies)	Interviewer encourages by nodding.
I: Anything else?	After the reply, a general prompt is supplied (PROMPT TYPE 2).
R: (no further reply)	

I: So how is this done in practice?

This is a *second main question,* shifting the focus from the authors' intentions to the respondent's own practice. As the respondent replies, the interviewer can mark off points on a check list, and then ask about those not covered.

R: ...

I: You've said how you use the quick quizzes. How do you use the end-of- section tests?

This is a probe for more detail on something the interviewee has mentioned (PROBE TYPE 1).

R: ...

I: So do you allocate pupils to levels once and for all, or might they change at the end of each section of the course?

This is a further probe, to expand and clarify the answer (PROBE TYPE 2).

By using the main questions to structure the interview, and planning the prompts and probes to guide it, you can decide how much control to exercise. In the example chosen, an alternative would be to let the interviewee decide on the 'key features' of the programme:

Interview	*Commentary*
I: I'd like to talk about what you see as the main innovative features of this programme, compared to what you were doing before ... OK?	Setting the scene and checking for understanding as before.
R: ...	
I: So could you identify one of the main features? ... Right ... What do you think they mean by that?	The *same first main question,* but on a feature chosen by the respondent.

The interviewer still creates the overall structure and can control how the features are discussed through the subordinate questions, just as in the first version.

Closed and open questions

An important aspect of control is the type of questions used. 'Closed' questions offer little scope in answering, and assert the interviewer's control: 'How many years have you been a principal teacher: less than two, from two to five, more than five?' Open questions offer a wide range of choice: 'Could you tell me about what you thought went well in this lesson?'.

Semi-structured interviews are likely to have a mixture of closed and open questions. Prompts are often open: 'Something you did, something they did, anything that you think went well', whereas probes usually close down the focus: 'What did you do during the lesson that helped that aspect of the lesson go well?'

Summary

The main characteristics of a semi-structured interview are:

- it is a formal encounter on an agreed subject, and 'on the record'
- main questions set by the interviewer create the overall structure
- prompts and probes fill in the structure: prompts by encouraging broad coverage, probes by exploring answers in depth
- there can be a mixture of closed and open questions
- the interviewee has a fair degree of freedom: what to talk about, how much to say, how to express it
- but the interviewer can assert control when necessary.

Let's now look at two other main types of interview.

Oral questionnaires

Chapter 1 referred to the highly structured interviews used in market research based on long checklists mostly of closed questions. Here the interviewer has very tight control and the person interviewed may feel uncomfortable about having so little free-dom of expression. Such an interview is like a postal question-naire, but done orally, and chapter 1 advised against it.

There are, however, some circumstances in which it is useful. If you are dealing with people who have difficulty in reading (young children, visually handicapped people, adult non-readers); or with people who may feel threatened by something that looks like an official form or a test (elderly people, disadvantaged groups, low achieving pupils or children with low attention span); or if you want to question people at a particular point in time or ensure a response from certain key informants, then you may find it nec-essary to ask the questions in person. In that case, think of it as an oral questionnaire, rather than an interview, and follow the prin-ciples of design, sampling and analysis outlined in books on ques-tionnaires.

Ethnographic interviewing
Ethnography is a style of research which you may also find re-ferred to as phenomenology, ethnomethodology or more loosely as qualitative research. The researcher works like an anthropolo-gist studying the way of life of a strange tribe. The aim is to see the world through the other person's eyes, to enter into their 'culture', to learn from them how they make sense of their experiences.

Small-scale ethnographic studies in education might focus on topics such as:
- school through the eyes of the beginning teacher
- the world of the habitual truant
- staffroom rituals and relationships
- how teachers and pupils negotiate informal classroom 'rules'.

Ethnography involves a special style of interviewing, which you may find labelled as ethnographic, naturalistic, non-directive or unstructured. A full discussion of this method would require an-other book: here we want to distinguish it from the semi- struc-tured technique.

In a semi-structured interview you create a structure mapping the topics to be covered, control the interview to ensure coverage and probe for reasons. In ethnography it is important to let the person being interviewed map out the topic. Main questions are therefore very open: 'Tell me about the kinds of things that people do in staff base'. Instead of probing to explore the interviewee's reasons, ethnographers probe to check their own understanding, often using their respondent's own language: 'Is that an example of what you call "mucking about"? What other kinds of "mucking about" are there?'

A key difference between semi-structured and ethnographic interviews is that in the former it is usually assumed that the interviewer and interviewee can share a common frame of reference. The structure that the interviewer creates should make sense to the other person, and so the interview can be a single business-like dialogue. In ethnography the interviewer is trying to find out the interviewee's frame of reference, and may have to work towards this slowly over a series of meetings.

Variations on semi-structured interviews

The semi-structured interview is capable of various adaptations.

Telephone interviews

These can provide access to key people whom it is difficult to meet: busy officials, or the remote members of a geographically widespread sample. The telephone has important limitations as a channel of communication. It is claimed that in face-to-face conversation 50% of the information exchanged is non-verbal, through posture, gesture and facial expression. This is missing when you interview by telephone, and you lose some of the advantages claimed in chapter 1. It is more difficult to sense whether someone is understanding your question. You can't offer non-verbal encouragement through smiles and nods. It is particularly difficult to interpret silence without non-verbal clues as to whether the other party is still involved in the dialogue.

Telephone interviewing requires techniques to sustain participation on both sides. The telephone seems to reduce the number of things people can deal with simultaneously. So, practise limiting the amount you say, and do not talk while the other person is talking. In place of body language you can use 'paralinguistic ut-terances' (yes, uh-uh, mmm, good) to give encouragement, but again, you should inject them into pauses rather than while the other person is speaking. Obviously, any visual material or printed prompts must be sent in advance, and you need to check that your interviewee has them handy.

Group interviews

In a group interview one interviewer talks to several people. Note-taking while guiding the group discussion is especially difficult and tape recording is probably essential. Even then, the recording may be noisy and confused. You need a good reason for choosing this kind of interview! One reason is that young children may be less inhibited if they meet an adult as a group. However, in any group discussion some people may dominate, and others contrib-ute little.

The most convincing reason for group interviews is that the group has some significance for your research. For example, if you are studying project work in the primary classroom, you might want to interview children in their working teams. If your interest is in decision-making at the departmental level in secondary schools, you might meet the departmental staff together. In both cases you are building into the interview the normal patterns of interaction within the group, and probably getting better evidence as a result. However, don't use groups with the aim of boosting the scale of your research. If you interview 150 people in groups of ten, your 'sample' is fifteen groups, not 150 individuals!

Summary

This chapter has tried to take some of the confusion out of the labels given to different types of interviews. It has discussed the main characteristics of the semi-structured interview, and con-trasted it with two others:

- *highly-structured interviews* as used in professional surveys, which are of little use in small-scale research except as an *oral questionnaire* in special cases.

- *ethnographic interviews* in which the researcher tries to understand another person's culture through a fairly lengthy non-directive approach.

The structure provided by the main questions allows semi-structured interviewing to be business-like. The variable control through the use of prompts and probes allows it to be flexible. Because of the possibility of a shared frame of reference, it is especially suitable for investigating professional concerns and issues in educational policy and practice. It can be used in a wide range of kinds of small-scale research: small-scale surveys, case studies, evaluations, action research projects, and in combination with classroom observation, in studies of teaching and learning. The technique is also useful outside the professional arena.

3

The Interview Schedule

Nothing is more important to the success of an interview study than having a good interview schedule. A schedule usually consists of several pages held on a clip-board. From this the interviewer reads out questions, marks off points covered, and occasionally makes extended notes. The schedule serves to guide the interview, to remind the interviewee of the formal nature of the discussion, and, once the interview is completed, may constitute an important part of the research evidence.

Even if you are used to giving lessons or lectures with a minimum of notes, you will find an interview schedule essential. At the most basic level, you need it to get through the interview without drying up, missing out questions, going off at a tangent, leading or confusing your respondent. The schedule is also important because it guarantees consistency of treatment across a set of interviews, which allows you to compare people's answers to questions which you have posed in the same way to everyone. (If more than one interviewer is sharing the work, then this becomes a key matter.) Finally, the interview schedule embodies the semi-structured framework you want (see Figure 1 opposite). It includes the main questions, the prompts and probes, and possibly short checklists to ensure coverage of important details. The successful structuring of the interview pays off when you come to the analysis.

Developing the schedule

In developing the schedule the starting point should be the research questions. These are the questions which guide your research by identifying the precise area of your investigation and the specific aspects that interest you. Research questions suggest the kind of information you need and how to collect it. The book-

SECTION 2 **What the authors mean**   NOTES

In this section I want to ask you about several of the features that the authors consider are important. I want to ask you about what you think they intend, and about how this works in practice.

Q2.1(a)   They say it provides a MULTI-LEVEL SCHEME
What do you think they mean by that?

prompt   "Pupils find their own level and work with appropriate extension material"

Q2.1(b)   How does this work in practice?

probe   use of check-tests   ☐

          section tests   ☐

          other evidence   ☐

          is allocation to a level permanent ☐
          or section by section?

Figure 1: Extract from a schedule for the interview discussed in Chapter 2.

let in this series *So You Want to Do Research?* by Lewis and Munn provides a guide to how to formulate research questions. Research questions should not be confused with the main questions you ask during the interview. There is of course a relationship between the two sets of questions: to answer your research questions you need to gather information and the interview questions are the mechanism for doing that. Let's look at an example.

Suppose that you have read that pupils' progress in maths often falters when they move from primary to secondary. You decide that this is worth investigating in local schools and devise a series of research questions based on possible explanations:

- is there evidence that pupils regress in mathematics in the early stages of secondary school?
- is there discontinuity between the primary and secondary curriculum in mathematics?
- are different teaching methods used in mathematics in primary and secondary schools?
- is there poor communication between primary and secondary schools about pupils' attainments in mathematics?

To answer these questions you could make use of evidence gathered in several ways: by testing pupils, by analysing syllabuses, by classroom observations of teaching, and by examining the contents of reports passed from primary to secondary. As part of the research you might want to interview teachers to find out whether they are aware of the problem, and if so, how they explain it, and what they think might be done about it.

You could of course ask teachers your research questions directly:

'Do you find that pupils "regress" in mathematics at the start of secondary school?'

'Are there important discontinuities between the primary and secondary curriculum?'

'Are there differences in teaching methods in primary and secondary schools?'

'Is there poor communication between the schools about pupils' attainments?'

However, this approach is likely to encourage people simply to rehearse their prejudices about the other sector.

Instead, you could ask questions to lead people into talking about things they know about, for example: 'What topics do you cover in the first term?' Then for each topic you could develop a probing sequence:

Main question: *Do pupils cover this in primary school?*

   (Probes):   How do you get to know about this?
                    Do all feeder schools cover it?
                    Do all pupils cover it?

Main question: *How do they teach this in primary school?*

   (Probes):   How do you get to know about this?
                    Is this different from what you do in secondary?
                    If so does this cause problems?

and so on. The research questions are being addressed indirectly.

Main questions

The main questions lead through your chosen topics. They should form a logical sequence, so that the interview 'flows' naturally. If you jump from one topic to another the interviewee may be confused and lose confidence in you.

As a rule you should place the more general questions first. You should avoid any sequence where the discussion of the first question is likely to influence later answers. Here is a sequence of topics from a study of teachers' reactions to aspects of the Curriculum 5-14 Programme in Scotland.

- What do you see as the main things 5–14 will require of you in the classroom?
- Will you make changes in your classroom organisation because of 5–14? Do you expect to make any changes in your teaching methods?
- Do you feel that some areas of the curriculum will become more important than at present?
- Thinking of your own class, how much differentiation will be needed and how will you provide it?

- Will the framework of outcomes and strands help you in relation to this? How will you approach assessment, and how will that change?

In this case the first question is the most open, inviting respondents to select what is in the forefront of their thinking. The interview then covers several aspects chosen by the researcher from a close reading of the official documents. Notice that you could not ask the first question at the end, because the answer would have been prompted by the earlier discussion, and would reflect the researcher's decision as to what are the important elements in the 5-14 programme.

This example shows some more subtle aspects of sequencing. *Changes in classroom organisation* are discussed generally before *curricular balance* or differentiation. Each of these might affect classroom organisation, and so if the order of questions were reversed, the interviewee might be influenced to talk about classroom organisation mainly in terms of these two aspects, having been 'prompted' unintentionally. The order in which differentiation, outcomes and assessment are tackled is possibly quite influential.

The present order may reflect the researcher's view: that the most important aspect is the differentiation of the curriculum to suit individual pupils; that to achieve that we need a framework with learning outcomes at different levels; and that as a result we have to provide differentiated assessment. An alternative view would be: that the first priority is to define clear standards for assessment and reporting; hence we need a framework of outcomes set at different levels; and the results of this assessment may require different levels of working within the curriculum. The question order chosen above may make it difficult for someone to communicate that different way of thinking.

The key point is that the order of your questions affects what people have in mind when they answer each one, and this can influence what they say. You need to think carefully about how you will sequence your schedule.

Keep the schedule simple

Sometimes you may want to let the interviewees decide the order in which they talk about topics (chapter 2 gives an example of this). In such a case you should try to have a standard prompting-and-probing routine for all topics they may bring up. You do not want to have to flip backwards and forwards mentally or even physically on your schedule, to find the relevant prompts, probes or checklists for each question.

Sometimes people create a branching structure in which they ask different sets of main questions in the light of previous answers. This can prove tricky. For example, it is often assumed that teachers can be divided into 'progressives' and 'traditionalists', or into 'child-centred' and 'subject-centred' groups, who have different ideas about the aims of education as well as about classroom practice. You might decide to investigate their views, using a few common questions to allocate people to the appropriate 'camp' and then following up with two different strands of questions for the different groups. If you do this you risk building preconceived ideas into the research. This might make it impossible for you to detect some very likely patterns, for example that there was a wide consensus on some matters, or as much variety within each group as between the groups. Even when the differences among interviewees are more objective (for example, some 'extract' pupils with learning difficulties, others do not; different schools have adopted different teaching programmes) it is usually best to have a single set of questions, allowing people to 'pass' on those that do not apply to them.

Prompts and probes

The purpose of prompts and probes is to help people say what they want to say. Prompts are directed towards what they know but have not yet mentioned. They encourage people to talk and jog their memory but they must not put words into people's mouths or pressurise the interviewees to come up with something. Probes are directed at what people have already said, asking them to clarify and explain, but not as a rule to justify or defend their position. (Leave confrontational interviewing to politics programmes on TV!)

There are some commonsense rules about the kinds of prompting you might use in different situations.

Prompts

- *If the person seems not to understand the question*

  Offer a specific prompt for that question: repeating the question in other words and possibly more fully, but don't suggest answers. Prompt 1 in chapter 2 shows an example.

- *If the person gives some answers and seems ready to continue*

  Offer a general prompt: 'any other (reasons/factors/advantages)?' as appropriate. Do this until they have finished, or do it a set number of times decided in advance.

- *If they appear to have finished*

  You may still want to check on other possibilities. You can offer specific prompts from a check-list on your schedule.

Both specific and general prompts should be planned into the schedule. They allow you to distinguish among:

- what is important to people (which they will mention without prompting)
- what they know about but don't regard as so important (which they may mention when prompted)
- what they don't know (which they will not say much about even after prompting from a check-list).

These distinctions may be important in relation to your research questions.

Probes

Whereas prompts invite different answers of the same kind, probes ask for an answer to be developed. It may be confirmed (they agree it is what they meant to say); clarified (they give more detail, express it more clearly); explained (they give the reasons behind what they said); connected (they show the link with something else mentioned earlier); or extended (linking to something they have not mentioned previously). Like prompting, probes can be general or specific. They should, however, be low-key and neutral, encouraging interviewees to expand on what they think but neither leading them nor challenging them. As with prompts, there are various stock situations.

Checking information

Interviewees may be imprecise: 'often', 'a lot', 'some of the staff'. You need to judge when and how to probe. If they tell you that 'most pupils can't be trusted to do homework' you would not ask them 'what proportion of pupils?' They are expressing a feeling, not a quantified judgement. If you want them to say more, you could offer a neutral probe by repeating what they say: 'You find you can't trust most pupils to do homework...' and pausing briefly. If they want to clarify, they will.

On other occasions a precise probe is indicated. 'You said you are short of time: that's with how many periods a week?' 'The Faculty: who is on the Faculty?'

Probing opinions, reasons, and feelings

This is often done by means of short probing sequences. These may begin by confirming and clarifying, and move on to explanations and connections. Often you can start by using the interviewee's own words. This helps keep the probing neutral.

'You say resources are a problem?' (confirming)

'What is it about resources that is the problem?' (clarifying)

'How does the resources problem affect the teaching?' (explaining, connecting)

For 'resources' you could substitute any factor mentioned as relevant to their teaching. There are many similar tactics you can use.

'So what you do at present is ... [in their own words]' (confirming)

'How do you do this at present?' (clarifying)

'How will that change in future?' (extending)

'How do you feel about the change?' (extending)

Again the wording of the probes is 'context-free'. This means that you can use the same probe repeatedly if necessary. It is also important as a way to keep the probing neutral and to avoid leading the interviewee.

The preamble

Every interview should begin with a preamble that reminds people of what they have agreed to, and what the interview is about. This allows any misunderstandings to be cleared up. When you first contact people you give them a general idea of the subject, but you may not want to say too much in case they talk to others or prepare their answers in advance (discussed in chapter 4).

The preamble lets you give a fuller explanation and establish the 'common frame of reference' which allows them to understand your questions in the way you intend. It is a good opportunity to clarify terms or ideas that are central to your study, for example:

> 'In my letter I said I am interested in teachers' use of informal assessment. By informal assessment I mean assessment that is not recorded or passed on to anyone else: that is the ways in which you check pupils' progress so that you can use this information yourself, mainly in today's lesson. For example it could include...'

The preamble may look quite lengthy on paper compared with the amount you would allow yourself to write at the start of a questionnaire about its subject-matter. However, it does not take long to speak it. You would not read it out in a solid chunk, but would pause, and use eye-contact to ensure that the interviewee is following what you say.

The first question

The first question is important. You can use it to set the right tone for the interview: they will do most of the talking; you will respond to what they say *in order to help them to say it*. The first question should allow them to talk at some length. It should not be threatening, and it should not be too important for the rest of the interview. It should allow you to judge what kind of respondent you have got (nervous, talkative, opinionated?).

Let us suppose that you are interested in teachers' views on truancy and the impact of new local authority guidelines. You will want to know whether people have read the guidelines, but you will not have said so in your letter, because that might send them off to read them when otherwise they might not. Your first question would not be 'Have you read the new local authority guidelines on truancy?' This is wrong in several ways. In the first place it does not allow them to talk much: the answer is likely to be 'Yes' 'No' or 'Well, I've had a look at them'. It seems to imply that you think they should have read them, that you consider such policy documents to be important. It may spoil rapport and give them a false idea of your own expectations. It would be better to start with a general question:

- As I said I am interested in truancy. Is this something that affects you? Are you aware of it in your work? Is it a problem for this school?

This tactic of using a small cluster of questions is useful for suggesting that you are interested in whatever they say, and are not looking for anything very specific. They can surely offer something. When you come to the question about the guidelines, you can soften it by using the same tactic:

- The authority has produced some new guidelines - did you know? Have you seen them? Have you had a chance to read them?

The final question

At the end of the interview you should ask a very open 'sweeper' question:

- Is there anything else you want to say about this topic, that I haven't asked you?

This is partly done as a matter of courtesy but also because the discussion may have stimulated the interviewer to think further about the topic. Then to round off:

- Is there anything else that you want to ask me?

They are likely to ask how your research is going and what you are finding out. You should be non-committal because they may talk to people you have still to interview!

And finally of course:

• Thank you very much for your time, that has been most interesting!

Wording the questions

This chapter has already included some specific suggestions about how to word questions. Perhaps the most fundamental point to remember is that an interview schedule is not a questionnaire: the people you interview never get to read it. Only you do that, and the test of the schedule is not how it reads on paper, but how it reads aloud when you use it to conduct an interview. As a beginner you are best to have a comprehensive schedule which you can stick to quite closely and fall back on easily at any time. Much of what you say during the interview may simply be read out from your schedule. As you plan your questions, speak them aloud to see if they sound natural.

A common mistake in wording is to go for absolute brevity and ask blunt, direct questions. This works in print but not in speech. The reason is that reading takes place in 'frozen time': people can pause to take stock, glance ahead, or look back at earlier points. Speech operates in 'real time' and you need to present people with information at a pace that allows them to absorb it, remembering that they cannot hold very much in mind at any one time while at the same time attending to what you might say next. You have to do some of the work for them by building into the interview at appropriate points a quick preview or recapitulation, and sufficient repetition and redundancy to ensure that they keep pace with you, and have in mind what you want them to have in mind at the point when you pose the question. You may have to prepare the question carefully, before you finally 'trigger' it:

'When I asked you about your problems as a student teacher, you mentioned the difficulty of fitting in with the teachers' routines. I'd like you to say more about that. For instance, suppose you are taking Mrs Simpson's class, and she is not actually in the room (OK, she would be nearby, but you don't expect she will come in.) In that situation, you might still feel there were quite a lot of things you would have to do her way .. uhuh .. what sorts of things?'

Using appropriate language

You should keep the language simple and appropriate to the people you are talking to. For example, whether you refer to 'geometry' or 'shape', to 'arithmetic', 'number work' or 'sums' may be the difference between being obscure and being patronising. You will of course want to avoid jargon, and not refer to 'effective curriculum delivery at classroom level' when you really mean 'good teaching'. But sometimes even 'teaching' needs to be defined precisely: are you asking people to include the preparation beforehand, and the marking of pupils' work afterwards? A phrase like 'less able pupils' may be interpreted as 'pupils in my bottom maths group', 'pupils with moderate learning difficulties' or 'pupils in the Foundation class'. You may want to avoid any of these meanings, and talk about 'the pupils who have not been getting on very well with this topic'.

Clear wording

You should avoid vague wordings: 'Do you give homework regularly?' (What counts as regularly? Once a year?) Here the questioner probably meant 'frequently'. It would be better to ask directly 'How often do you give homework?' Negatives, and especially double negatives, are to be avoided: 'Is it unusual for pupils not to have homework?' is confusing because of the implied negative of 'unusual' and the explicit negative of 'not'. 'Do pupils have homework most evenings?' is easier to follow.

A question such as:

> 'What are your views on the mainstreaming of pupils with learning difficulties, or with behavioural problems, in the later years of secondary education?'

is full of faults. 'Mainstreaming' may be an unfamiliar term, and besides it may mean different things to different people. Also the question is 'double-barrelled': it refers to two groups of pupils. People may have different ideas about these groups but the question does not seem to allow this. Again, what exactly is meant by 'the later years'? And of course the question is too long and complicated. The interviewee will have forgotten the beginning before the interviewer has reached the end.

Leading questions

Books on interviewing emphasise the danger of unintentionally leading people towards a particular answer. The mere fact that you want to interview them about something suggests that you regard it as important, and they will try to appear knowledgeable and interested. It has been well established that interviewees try to express views that they think the interviewer wants to hear. For that reason the preamble might avoid emphasising the importance of the topic ('Truancy is a problem that affect us all in education') in favour of stressing your interest in their views ('I am interested to know how far this is something that affects you..')

In wording questions, you should obviously avoid phrases like 'Do you think that...?', and even more 'Do you agree that...?' You should also beware of offering people a limited choice: 'Do you prefer the phonetic approach, or 'look-and-say'?' presses them to take sides (many teachers would say they prefer to use both). 'Do you use visual aids such as slides, overheads or videos?' is likely to produce a response in terms of these three devices only. 'How do you implement the communicative approach in language teaching?' or 'Do you differentiate mainly through group work or through individualisation?' assumes that these approaches are being used, or suggests that they should be.

Fact and fiction

In order to please you, people may try to answer questions even when they lack any relevant knowledge or experience, and you should word your questions to try to detect or prevent this. You can quickly ask what they know about something, before asking what they think about it, or how they feel as a result of their experience of it. For example, if you are seeking their views on the fairness of promotion interviews, you can ask when they were last involved, so that you can distinguish between views based on recent experience and others based on staff-room speculation.

It is quite common for informants to misremember facts, and tell you, for example, that Tessa got over 70 in her test, when in fact she got a good deal less. This probably does not matter: more important is the 'fact' that the teacher thinks Tessa did well. You would not challenge this during an interview, nor would you use an interview to collect information which would be better obtained from the marks book either before or afterwards.

Layout

The schedule is a working document. It must be easy to use, and you should consider carefully how to lay it out, and try different versions if necessary. The print should be big enough that you can read it easily if it is lying on your lap, and you can use boxes, lines, and other devices to make it easy to distinguish between sections and pick out the key questions. It is common to set the text out in columns, one for the main questions, another for the prompts and probes, with a place to tick off items as they are covered and space to make notes. You may need to turn the page on its side to get enough room. (See page 19 for an example.)

Shredding and piloting

Once you are satisfied with your schedule you should get one or two colleagues to 'shred' it with you, looking for the kinds of faults just discussed. Ask the 'shredders' to imagine how the interviewee will react to and interpret the questions. Choose people who are likely to be sympathetic to your work but willing to give forthright comments and precise criticism. Don't use people who are involved in the research. They are likely to be too immersed in your way of thinking and talking to provide a detached critique. In shredding you should not try to defend your wording or persuade others to accept that it is best. Rather you should try to meet all their criticisms, since at least some of the interviewees may react to the questions in these various ways.

You should also test your schedule in some pilot interviews. Piloting is discussed in detail in chapter 5. It involves recording interviews with people who are not part of your sample. You then play back the interviews so that the interviewees can comment on whether the questions 'worked', and allowed them to say what they intended. Piloting also allows you to find out how long the interview takes, and to evaluate your own ability to make the schedule work. If you decide to modify the schedule, further piloting may be advisable.

Summary

This chapter has emphasised the importance of the interview schedule. These are some of the main points to remember:

- The schedule questions are derived from your research questions, but are not the same as them
- The schedule creates the structure you want, and gives you the degree of control you need
- Keep the schedule simple, using general purpose prompts and probes when possible
- In wording the questions, remember you are planning for the spoken not the written word
- The test of your schedule is how it works as an interview: hence piloting is vital.

4

Planning and Preparation

The topic, and the particular research questions you have in mind, will determine the kind of information you need and the kinds of people you should interview. The decision about how many, and which, individuals to approach must be made carefully. Amongst other things it depends on whether you see your investigation more as a survey or as a case study.

In a survey the aim is to ask lots of people the same questions in the same way, so as to obtain standardised information. From this you can look at similarities and differences among groups and individuals, and across questions.

If the 'population' to be surveyed is large (all probationer teachers, all parents of pupils with hearing difficulties) then you have to select a sample. This raises the question of whether the information you get is typical of what you would have found if you had been able to question everybody. You cannot know this but, provided you have used proper sampling methods, statistical calculation will allow you to estimate the likelihood of any significant difference between the sample and the population as a whole. This tells you the degree of confidence with which you can assert your findings. The bigger the sample, the more confident you can be. Unfortunately using semi-structured interviews you cannot cover a big sample, and statistical confidence levels will be low.

One way out of this is to restrict your selected 'population' and the claims you aim to make, so that sampling becomes unnecessary. For a great many small-scale studies this is not a serious restriction because they do not aim to find universal truths but simply to get sound information and understanding about their local context. Let's suppose that you are interested in mathematics teachers' views on their needs in in-service training. You cannot interview all the mathematics teachers in the country, or even in your local authority. However, you could decide to focus on a smaller group, on the grounds that their needs are probably distinctive: say probationary teachers, or newly appointed heads of department. Then you can aim to cover all such people in the authority, and will not need to sample. You might call your report 'In-service Needs of Probationary Maths Teachers (or 'New Heads of Maths'): a Survey in One Local Authority'.

Alternatively, you could interview all the mathematics teachers in two schools. Here you could aim to find out how people's views on their in-service needs reflect the particular circumstances in which they work. Again you avoid the need to sample. Your report might be entitled 'In-service Needs in Context: Case Studies of Two Mathematics Departments'. The phrase 'case studies' emphasises that you are dealing with two particular examples, and are not making any claims that these schools are typical. People may think they recognise similarities with their own schools, but they need to test these out for themselves.

If the differences between schools are likely to be significant, then you might think: why not spread the interviews to include, say, four teachers in each of five schools? If you do, then there are both gains and losses.

You lose in confidence about the picture in any one school. You now have to sample each school, and you cannot be sure that your four teachers are typical of the whole staff. For example, if three say one thing, and the fourth the opposite, you cannot claim that you know the majority view. If you had selected even one person in your sample differently, you might have found apparent unanimity, or an even split. With such small numbers, individuals become significant. If your group happens to include a probationer or part-time teacher, or to exclude the head of department, then this affects what you can say confidently about this school.

By sacrificing certainty about individual schools, you have gained better information about the differences across schools. However, a 'sample' of five schools out of possibly 30 does not constitute a 'survey' of the schools in the local authority. You have simply got five linked case studies, and each should be reported as a unique portrait. If there are common features or important differences you can highlight them in these accounts but, as a rule, you will not be able to prove their significance statistically.

Random sampling

Even though statistical tests are not likely to be a feature of small-scale studies based on semi-structured interviews, the principle of random sampling is still useful. Take the example of selecting your five schools from 30. You might be tempted to construct a 'sample' deliberately, to represent a 'typical' range of schools: large, medium, and small, or with good, average and poor catchment areas. However, it is not obvious that the size of a school, or its catchment area, should affect the mathematics staff's in-service needs. The range you are building in is probably irrelevant to your research. You would be better to select schools at random.

Similarly in choosing the four teachers, you could again select at random. However, it would seem strange if you missed out the head of department or whoever else had special responsibility for staff development. In such cases, your group of four interviewees would be the head of department plus three others selected at random.

Random sampling is straightforward. With small numbers, you can simply draw names out of a hat! More usually you make a numbered list of the individuals eligible to be interviewed. Use a table of random numbers, or generate them from a microcomputer, and select people from the list accordingly until you have as many as you need. It is as well to select some 'reserves' in case people decline to be interviewed.

Quota sampling

The departure from strict random sampling in this case is justified on theoretical grounds: by obvious relevance to the topic of the research. You can take this principle further. For example, if you are studying the impact of an organisational innovation (for example, the devolution of financial planning to schools, or the impact of 'incorporation' in further education colleges) you might predict that the effects will vary with individuals' levels of management responsibilities, and so divide your interviews into groups based on people's positions in the hierarchy, allocating a quota of interviews to each. A plan for a case study in one institution might look like this.

Group 1:   Management team
           Interview all members, since each
           has unique responsibilities   6 interviews

Groups 2, 3, 4:   Teaching staff
                  Interview a sample at each of three
                  levels of promotion

           (Group 2)   Heads of department   4 interviews
           (Group 3)   Other promoted staff   4 interviews
           (Group 4)   Unpromoted staff   6 interviews

Here the quotas of interviews are not proportional to the numbers of people in that group. In Group 1, because it has a special significance, we interview everyone. Otherwise there is a sliding scale: four interviews to give a spread in each group, and some extra interviews if the category is especially numerous or varied. This should produce a well-rounded case study. It is clearly no longer a survey in which you treat everyone as equivalent and ask them all the same questions. You may have different interview schedules for people at different positions in the hierarchy.

Snowball sampling

So far we have looked at examples in which the researcher selects the people to interview. A different approach which is especially useful in case studies is to collect names through 'snowball sampling'. First, you identify a few key informants: the main people involved in the activity you are studying. When you approach them or interview them, you ask them to suggest other people to whom you should speak to gain a full and balanced picture. This gives you a second outer group. You can use the same process with them and add a third layer to your 'snowball'. The 'snowballing' can continue until you find you are not getting any new names, in which case you can feel confident that you have interviewed the people most central to your research. On the other hand, you may have to stop because you have as many people as you can possibly interview, in which case you must hope that you have covered the most important people. You may have to adapt your interviews to individuals because they have been chosen for different reasons: your 'snowball' is a collection, rather than a sample.

Avoiding bias

This section has emphasised the need to have some principle on which you select your interviewees. This is to avoid the criticism that your sample is biased in some way: that you have chosen people who are different from others in some respect that is obviously relevant to the topic of your research, and so casts doubt on your findings. People will always question whether your sample is 'truly representative'. No-one can ever prove whether it is, unless they are prepared to survey the whole of your population. What you can do is to show that you have not introduced a systematic bias through your choice of respondents.

Bias becomes an issue if you ask people to volunteer to be interviewed. This should ensure that you have cooperative interviewees who have something to say, but the danger is that you meet only the enthusiasts or the entrenched opposition. Volunteers are useful for piloting, or for a purely exploratory study when you want to get a lot of information quickly in order to plan a more thorough investigation. Otherwise it is better if you select the people you want, and encourage them to take part, while recognising their right to opt out.

When you have assembled your list of intended interviewees it is worth while to look at it with bias in mind. Because you are dealing with small numbers, the process of random choice might have given you a selection that looks obviously lop-sided, and is liable to be criticised. If so, you could repeat the whole process. Or you may simply plan how to live with the criticism.

Summary

This section has discussed the decisions you have to consider when deciding whom to interview:

- decide what kinds of people you need to interview
- decide how many people you can afford to interview
- decide whether you will
  - treat the interviews as one group (a small-scale survey)
  - or divide them into more than one group for some reason connected with the focus of your research questions
  - or treat them as a collection of individual interviews
- within each group
  - interview everyone if you can
  - otherwise sample within the group at random
  - or collect individuals by 'snowballing'
- finally look at your list of interviewees with the criticism of bias in mind.

Approaching your interviewees

Once you have selected the people you wish to talk to, you must get them to agree to be interviewed. You will also need permission from their superiors. Let's look first at what's in it for the interviewees. What can you offer them in return for their help?

Some research may in principle offer a tangible reward. For example you might be studying an acknowledged problem, such as how to introduce a new element (media studies, or a 'European dimension') into an already crowded timetable. An action research strategy could help the school to achieve this while allowing the researcher to study the difficulties to be overcome. Or you might carry out a set of case studies showing how schools in different circumstances have introduced these changes, which could help these schools to learn from others' experiences. Sometimes schools will be keen to collaborate because they hope to gain some good publicity from the report (this may conflict with the usual rules about confidentiality). Individuals may be attracted by the chance to have their say anonymously on some contentious issue such as

National Testing, possibly with the hope that the research may influence policy.

Unfortunately these benefits are usually speculative. You cannot guarantee them, and you should be cautious about making promises. Usually you don't need to. Many people will welcome the interview for the simplest of motives: it is a chance to talk to someone outside their network of (often pressurised) professional relationships, someone who is interested in their views and in what they are doing, and who will listen intelligently and sympathetically, and report honestly. This is something you can promise (otherwise you should not be doing the research!). You need to convey this by the manner of your approach rather than by stating it. Be open about your intentions, avoid antagonising or misleading people, and give a general impression that you know what you are doing.

In particular you should make clear the practical demands on them if they take part. This will include the time taken up by the interview itself. You should estimate this accurately, and stick to it when the time comes. If you intend tape-recording, get their agreement: mention it as being in the interest of accuracy. Make clear how flexible you can be about when and where the interview can take place. In addition you may ask them for some of the following:

- to do some preparation (for example looking out relevant documents)
- to allow a follow-up phone call or letter to check anything that is not clear from the interview record
- to read and comment on a summary or transcript of their interview
- to read and comment on your draft research report.

Everything should be anticipated and negotiated at the start.

Making the approach

The approach may be made by letter, by telephone or by a visit, depending on who you are dealing with, but you must always at some point put the details of your request in writing. With colleagues in schools you might use a phone call to clear the ground, followed by a letter firming up the details. With busy officials it is often better to send the letter first, promising that you will follow up by telephone in about ten days time. Make sure too that people have your phone number in case they have to cancel at short notice.

Your letter should cover a number of points, for example:

Who are you and what you are interested in?
> 'I am a primary school teacher working mostly with P6 and P7. I am interested in the value of out-of-school visits in the teaching of environmental studies for this age group.'

Why have you contacted this person in particular?
This is easy if the person has special relevance to your research:
> 'I am contacting you because of your work in developing material for the Museums service.'

It is more difficult if they are part of random sample. You need to express this positively!
> 'My aim is to get the views of a wide range of class teachers based on their different experiences.'

What do you want them to do for you?
> 'I would like to visit your school to talk to you either during school hours or after school. The interview would take less than an hour. At the same time I should be interested in seeing any material you use to support out-of-school visits.'

Why are you doing the research and for whom?
> 'I have received permission from the Region to contact schools. However, this is a personal piece of research and is not carried out on behalf of any official body or as part of any course that I am taking.'

A guarantee of confidentiality and a promise of feedback
> 'No material relating to the interview will be accessible to anyone other than myself. In reporting the work I will ensure that

individuals and schools remain anonymous. I shall send you a brief summary of my findings once the research is completed [by December] and hope that you find it helpful in your work.'

How much do you tell them?

You need to tell people something about the subject matter of the interview. If they are to agree to meet you, they need to feel confident that they can contribute something useful and that your questions will not take them uncomfortably by surprise. You need to know this too, and not discover during the interview that you have assumed knowledge or experience that they just do not have: they don't teach health studies or don't have any bilingual pupils. To avoid these problems you can indicate the broad areas to be covered. However, as a rule you would not reveal the main questions. You want the interview to unfold naturally, and you do not want them to read up, talk to others and prepare answers in advance.

A possible exception to this occurs if you are interviewing someone in a policy-making position and you want them to give you a considered 'official' view. You may submit the main questions in advance. Indeed they may insist on that.

Negotiating with authorities

As well as getting the agreement of the people you want to interview, you are likely to need permission from their superiors in the educational hierarchy. This has the curious effect that the more important the person, the simpler the negotiation. If you wish to interview the Director of Education, you need only the Director's permission.

If you want to interview pupils, then several stages are involved:

- you need the education authority's permission to approach the school
- you need the head teacher's permission to work in the school
- you need the class teacher's permission
- you need the parents' permission (the school will usually contact them for you).

The pupils' permission is often taken for granted! However, you might visit the school and explain your research to the pupils and give them the chance to opt in or out.

You may wonder whether this rigmarole is necessary when all you want is to talk to a few people. You may already know your interviewees professionally. Why not meet them after school, off the premises? Surely it is no-one's business what people talk about in their spare time? Or perhaps you can integrate your research with normal professional activities, such as staff development, which are happening anyway?

To answer this question we need to understand the concerns of education authorities and head teachers. In general, they want to know who is going in and out of their schools and what these people are doing. More specifically, the local authority and head teachers have to guarantee that teachers' time is not being wasted and that pupils' education is not being interrupted. Also, they wish to avoid any bad publicity for the school or authority. At some point your research will be published, and those in positions of responsibility want to anticipate the kinds of findings you might report and how these may be interpreted and represented by others. You may give a positive account of a school's successful initiative to counter racism, glue-sniffing or bullying: the effect may be to alarm parents about problems of which they were previously unaware.

Whether you need permission and whether you get it obviously depends on the topic and style of your research. In general it makes sense to seek formal permission. You cannot keep the research secret and if you are caught in the act then you may be stopped and other researchers may find it more difficult to get permission in future. If you cannot reassure the authority about these matters, then you should consider very carefully whether you should be doing this research.

The process of negotiation can be slow. There can be wide variations depending on the locality and the time of year, and it is useful to ask someone who has been in your position how long it took in their case. Fortunately, you can save time if you move simultaneously at different levels. For example, you can approach the teachers initially by telephone. If they express interest, confirm the details of your request to them in writing, and also write to the school and the authority, stating that you have informal agreement from the teachers, and are now formally seeking permission at these other levels. Where relevant a covering letter from the supervisor or director of your research should be included. Nowadays local authorities may have a senior member of their administrative staff who deals with research requests, and there may be an official application form. You can check the exact procedure by telephone.

Your letter to the local authority and others should cover the same points as that to your interviewees. It should be as short and businesslike as possible. You should be precise about how the research will be reported and to whom, and offer to send a copy of the report to the authority. (They may be interested in assisting its dissemination.)

Dealing with problems

Some problems may arise during the negotiation. You may be asked to provide a copy of your interview schedule. This would imply that you have to do all the work of developing the schedule without knowing whether the research can take place at all, and also, having to reveal your detailed questions in advance of the interview. You should try to pre-empt this problem, by explaining that your interviews are to be semi-structured and are not prescripted in detail. Send a list of the topics to be covered as you would to your interviewees. This is usually acceptable, and it allows you to complete the development and piloting of the schedule while you are waiting for permission.

Sometimes if the topic is of special interest to the authority you may receive suggestions for changes in your interview. These can be acknowledged, and dealt with in the same way as other issues that arise during shredding and piloting, as described in chapter 3. If the changes are insisted on as a condition of giving permission, then you need to decide whether they are compatible with your research goals.

Planning a round of interviews

In planning your complete set of interviews you need to make a realistic estimate of the time required. The interview itself will take about an hour to which you must add time for travelling and for chatting to people before and afterwards. You are unlikely to be able to arrange two interviews end-on, and should reckon on needing a morning, afternoon or evening for each interview. Similarly you cannot expect to cover the round of interviews on successive half-days. The logistics of matching your free time with others' may be complicated, and some interviews may be cancelled because of unforeseeable events. You may find that two or three interviews a week is as much as you can manage. However, this allows you to do some work on them and check for any problems with the recording or the interviewing technique.

Because the interviews are spread out in time they do not all take place against the same background. Depending on your topic it may matter if some of them occur before the examinations or the Easter holidays, and some after. Your own knowledge of the events and rhythms of the school year should allow you to avoid any major discrepancies between the circumstances of the first and last interviews. However, you may still fall victim to unpredictable events, such as the announcement of a pay settlement, or the issue or non-issue of an important policy paper.

It is best to confine your interviewing to as short a block of time as possible, and not to attempt too much. A single term is a good period to choose.

The interview setting

It is normal practice for you to travel to your interviewees. This is partly a matter of courtesy, since they are doing you a favour. It is also beneficial to the interview itself, because it takes place in the natural context of the activities you are going to discuss. This should have a general influence of making the discussion more realistic. It also allows people to point out things rather than describing them: here is where they work with the computer, this is the kind of record that is kept of which packages are used. This can happen during an interview conducted in situ, or during a quick look round before or afterwards. The notes you make can be added to the interview record.

You may also gain an impression of the overall context: whether the school seems well resourced, staff morale high, the pupils well behaved. You can make notes on these points too. These notes may help you later in interpreting your interview material, but they should be used with caution. They are your ideas, not those of your informants, and so they do not have the same status as the data you get in the interview itself.

Information about the context can therefore enrich that from the interview. The context can also influence the interview, and there are pitfalls. Some settings are threatening. The guidance base, the head teacher's office, the medical room, may all carry reminders of other conversations that may inhibit pupils, staff or parents! Official-looking settings may be off-putting to people from disadvantaged groups. Teachers interviewed across a large desk may unwittingly adopt the style and language of policy documents, as if they were at a committee meeting or a promotion interview.

People will talk with more confidence on their own territory and this is one reason for you to go to your interviewees. In some cases there is a risk of them becoming too confident and taking over the interview, and so you may want a more neutral setting: interviewing teachers in the general staffroom rather than their own classrooms for instance. With parents, whether you meet them in the school, in their home, or elsewhere, may make a difference to their willingness to talk, and what they say.

The presence of others is a significant factor. Young children may need the reassurance of having parents or friends present. Adolescents are strongly influenced by their peers and may feel obliged to adopt a flippant or anti-school manner which they would not do if on their own.

Practical considerations

In choosing the setting, try to ensure that the interview will not be disturbed by people coming in and out or the interviewee being called away to the telephone. Avoid extraneous noise. The human ear can focus on what people are saying but the tape recorder cannot and will pick up noise from the class next door, workmen on the roof, and vibrations affecting the table on which it is placed.

It is best not to face your respondent directly: it suggests confrontation. Do not sit beside them either: they cannot resist trying to read your schedule! Two arrangements seem to work well. Either sit up at adjacent sides of a table, on which you can place the tape recorder and any papers, or else sit back in two easy chairs placed at an angle of about 120 degrees, with a low table nearby for the recorder, and your schedule on your lap. These positions allow you to use eye contact, making, sustaining and breaking it off when you want to, and to be able to write (or appear to write) without the interviewee trying to read it. It is also good to have a nearby mains point for your tape recorder, which avoids any worries about batteries going flat.

These are all counsels of perfection. Since you are not on your home ground you have to settle for what you can get. It is not unknown for a teacher to propose holding the interview in the classroom: 'It's all right, I'll just give the class something to get on with while we talk'!

Tape recording

A wide range of tape recorders can be used for interview work. Since you are concerned with speech rather than music, hi-fi is not necessary. The latest miniature model is not necessarily the best: I prefer an older machine which is heavier but sturdier, and has good large controls. What is important is to get to know your recorder. Practise with it at home, and develop a standard routine for setting it up and using it. In particular, practise positioning the recorder or microphone for best results. You should know how to point it and how far to place it from the interviewee and from yourself, depending on whether the voice is louder or softer than average. Sometimes interviewers like to start by dictating the time and place of the interview on to the tape, or asking the interviewee to say something, so as to check that the recording is working at the right level. However, this draws attention to the recorder, and you may prefer to avoid it.

Remember that your interview data is precious, and do not put it at risk by false economies. Use a fresh tape each time (C60 or C90 are less prone to snarl up than the thinner C120) and as soon as the interview is finished, write the details on the tape and remove the record-protect tab, so that you cannot erase it by mistake. Never chance running a recorder on tired batteries. Always carry spares, and if in doubt, replace. Use mains electricity whenever you can.

Finally, two problems that you may encounter: first, some recorders have controls that can get shifted while they are being carried. You may be able to use sticky tape to keep them at their normal settings. Second, you may want to carry a soft pad on which to place the recorder or microphone, so that it does not pick up vibrations from surroundings.

Summary

In making arrangements you quickly realise that your interviews are more important to you than anyone else. Others do not share your sense of urgency. You have to plan for the 'worst case scenario' in which anything that can go wrong, does. So...

- Start early on making arrangements and seeking permission. It will take twice as long as you expect.
- Plan the interviews within a block of time, say 6–12 weeks. Recognise that you cannot expect to fit them together efficiently, and reckon on some having to be postponed at the last minute.
- Use the telephone for initial contact and to remind people, but make sure your request is also put fully in writing.
- Be honest about what you are going to do, and what you want of them. Tell them only as much as they need to know, and tell everyone the same.
- Expect to have to travel to them. Do what you can to create a suitable setting for the interview.

In this chapter we have looked at some stages in preparing for the interviews. None of these is especially difficult or time-consuming, or requires special skill. It is more a matter of thinking carefully and attending to detail. Don't be tempted to skimp on them or cut corners. Each stage makes a necessary contribution to the success and soundness of the study.

5

Doing the Interview

The preceding chapters have been about planning and preparation. Now we come to the real thing, the interview itself. You may be surprised to find that this is not one of the longer chapters!

One reason for this is that it is easy to overdo talk about 'interviewing skills', and create a mystique about interviewing, stressing the difficulty of simultaneously maintaining the flow by verbal and non-verbal means, absorbing information and remembering what has been covered, noting points to probe and follow up, and taking notes, in the interviewee's own words whenever possible.

This would indeed demand a lot of skill, but it is not necessary. The approach taken in this book emphasises preparation rather than improvisation. Develop a simple schedule and stick to it, word questions naturally and use a tape recorder, and you will not depend heavily on interviewing skills. When beginners get into difficulties it is most often because they feel obliged to 'get involved' in the interview. As a result they talk too much and so get drawn off the schedule or start leading their respondents. By contrast others get excellent results by a 'minimalist' approach, doing little more than read out their series of main questions from the schedule. You are probably much better to think about 'how to keep this interview manageable', rather than becoming concerned about general interviewing skills.

In any case, you cannot learn oral skills purely from a book. That needs practice and constructive feedback. What the book can do is help you to have a clear idea of what you are trying to do when interviewing, suggest some mechanisms for getting feedback and point out what to look for when monitoring your own performance. In a successful interview, you get your data. The interviewees get to state their case. For both purposes it is what they say that matters. Anything you contribute is simply to help them put on record what they know, think and feel about the agreed topics. Because of this an interview is a joint venture, but it is not symmetrical. You do not have to 'take turns' and hold up one end of the dialogue, as you would in a conversation, and you should not be drawn into doing so. You can help avoid this if you think carefully about how you will 'present' yourself at the start of the interview.

Presenting yourself

When we meet someone for the first time we quickly size them up and thereafter we talk to them in a way we think they will understand and find acceptable. Indeed very often we talk to them in the way we think they expect of us.

These interpersonal factors obviously affect any interview. People's willingness to talk to you, and what people say to you, is influenced by who they think you are: this includes their notion of your official position, and of the kind of person they take you to be. For that reason it is worthwhile to give some thought to how you will dress and the general manner you will adopt at the interview. There is plenty of evidence that an interview can be distorted by significant differences between the parties involved, in age, race, sex, wealth or status. This is all the more likely if the subject under discussion is a sensitive and personal one. So, if a white researcher interviews black people about racial harassment, or a middle-aged woman asks teenage boys about their sexual behaviour, the interviews are likely to be difficult, and it would be naive to assume that the respondents' answers represent the whole unvarnished truth. It is questionable whether semi-structured interviewing is an appropriate method of gathering information in these extreme cases.

Fortunately in most cases you will be interviewing people with whom you share important common ground: perhaps a professional relationship, or a common interest in their children's education, so that social differences are not the major consideration. It is not worth while trying to disguise them. (You may find it difficult to sustain the disguise, and that certainly would be damaging.) You can avoid exacerbating them, or presenting yourself in a way that might irritate people. An interview is not the occasion to make a strong personal statement in your dress and manner! Rather you should aim to appear fairly anonymous but friendly; tidy and businesslike, but not aggressively smart.

Maintaining distance

Ethnographic researchers often take some trouble to blend in and identify with their respondents, but in semi-structured interviewing it is often better to maintain some 'distance' between yourself and the interviewee. Then people will realise that they have to explain things, and will not be surprised if you betray ignorance or ask a naive question. It is tempting to invoke solidarity by saying 'I used to teach in a school just like this' or 'I have two boys at secondary school myself' but it may be counterproductive.

'Maintaining distance' does not imply being aloof. You have to assure people of a sympathetic hearing. It does mean making it clear that the two of you have different and complementary roles in this interview. In particular, your task is to understand their viewpoint, not to evaluate it, and so you may say 'Yes, I understand' or 'I see what you mean' but not 'Yes, that's right' or 'I do so agree with you'.

Interviewees are likely to assume that you are knowledgeable about the topic, and maybe that you hold a strong point of view. They may be anxious to know what that view is before they commit themselves. Resist any suggestion that you are an expert, and emphasise that you are doing research in order to find out about the topic, and have not yet formed a view. If they ask what you have been finding out from the interviews, say that you have not done many so far.

They may also assume that you are an experienced interviewer. Try to live up to this expectation, so as to give them confidence in the exercise. Above all do not feel self-conscious about referring to your schedule. By doing so, you remind them that this is 'on the record', a formal meeting to which you are both committed, and which you aim to ensure is carried out according to plan.

Difficult cases

It is often difficult to interview close colleagues. For one thing they may take it for granted that you share a body of common knowledge and experience, and so may not mention it in their answers. You may have to remind them to do so, even if it seems rather silly at the time. Otherwise it will not appear in the record. Another difficulty occurs if they assume that you share their views, or if they know very well that you do not. This can create tension during the interview – or later.

In such cases you can emphasise the formality of the interview, making play of using the schedule, and so on. Aim to convey that you are duty bound to ask the same questions of them as of anyone else, and in the same way; that they should answer accordingly, and that their answers will remain confidential, that is, only to be used for the purposes of your research.

Pupils also count as difficult cases. They usually regard any adult asking them questions as 'some sort of a teacher', and are quick to penetrate any pretence that you are not! This means that their response is affected by expectations derived from the classroom (is this a sort of test? are they supposed to know the answers?) and notions of what it is proper to say to teachers. The best you can do is to run your interview formally, treat their answers seriously, and show neither approval nor disapproval of the views they express. In interpreting the results, you need to bear in mind that what you have got is not 'pupils' views' so much as 'statements made by pupils in an interview with a (supposed) teacher'. You should not attempt to make allowance for this, or reinterpret what they have said, even if – especially if! – they are your own pupils.

Conducting the interview

It is up to you to 'conduct' the interview so as to bring it to a successful conclusion in the time agreed. You need to develop tactics for encouraging people to talk, moving them on through the questions, getting them to stop and think, and keeping them on the subject. Some of these are now discussed.

Non-verbal devices

Non-verbal tactics have the advantage that they do not interfere with the substance of what is being said, and so do not 'lead' the interviewee undesirably. It is difficult to be aware of your non-verbal behaviour and to use it systematically, so the following points illustrate what is possible, rather than prescribe a method.

Eye contact is useful. In British society it is rude to stare fixedly at someone or to avoid looking at them at all while you are talking with them. You want to maintain intermittent eye contact with the interviewee, and the schedule can provide a useful 'prop'. When asking a question you can read from the schedule, then look up to check that the interviewee has understood and is ready to answer. Then you can break the contact by looking down to take notes (or even just pretending to take notes), nodding and glancing up occasionally to show that you are following. When the interviewee stops talking, if you avoid eye contact they may be encouraged to continue, while if you look up it can signal that you are ready to ask something else.

Timing is important. It is considered impolite to interrupt or jump in too quickly after someone has spoken, but you may have to do this to keep the interview on course. You can use a non-verbal signal to warn them that you are about to intervene, and so soften the effect. As well as using eye contact, you can use gestures, such as holding your hand up to stop them talking if you have not finished your question, or if they have misunderstood, or if you want to probe something. You can 'sit back' to signify that you are ready to listen to an extended answer. I sometimes use a gesture as if handing something to the interviewee, to signal 'I'm finished, it's all yours'.

Tone of voice or pace of speech can be varied: speak briskly to indicate 'This is a simple factual question to be dealt with quickly' or more slowly to suggest 'This needs thought and I am prepared to wait for a considered answer.'

Verbal tactics

People develop stock phrases to manage their interviews. To encourage people to talk you will probably find yourself saying

'Good' 'Right' 'Yes' 'OK' 'Fine' 'Yes that's interesting' all the way through. It sounds awful on the tape, but it is good tactics!

If they are long-winded you may want to speed up the interview but this can be tricky. You may be tempted into unscheduled prompting that 'leads' their answers, or to abandon necessary probes, or even to cut short an answer after making a premature decision that you know what they are going to say. If you do intervene, soften it: 'Good, I've got that, can we leave it there for the moment? – because we can come back to it later ...'

Most people do try to answer your questions, and it is best to assume that whatever they say, they see it as relevant. Sometimes they seem to be wandering off, but then make a connection with the question at the very end of their answer. If you find that they really do lose the thread, you can stop them: 'OK, this is obviously important – but I want to be sure how it relates to (say) the level of resources?' (and if it does not) 'Well, let's leave it, we can come back to your point later ...'

There are ways in which you can aim to save time if the interview is taking too long. You can announce (when appropriate) 'The next few questions only need short answers'. Remember too that if you don't entirely follow an answer, it is not always necessary to probe it there and then. You have the answer in full on the tape, and can listen to it carefully as often as you need.

If people have clearly misunderstood the question then stop them, politely. Always blame yourself. Don't say 'That's not what I meant ...' but 'I'm sorry, I didn't ask that right ...' If they do not answer, or say they cannot understand the question, then often it is enough to repeat the question, watching to see where they have difficulty, and wait. Otherwise you may be drawn into an unprepared prompt that in retrospect can be seen as 'leading' their answer. If they still cannot answer, then you can say 'Fine, let's leave it, if it doesn't ring a bell. I must not force people into an answer.'

If you have been working your interviewee hard, you may decide to allow a breather. One way is to say 'Right, let's check over what we have covered in that last section'. You can then skim over the last few questions, mentioning some of the points they made, and which you have noted on the schedule. This device for making a break also gives them confidence that they have said something substantial, and that you have been listening, and getting it on the record. They may be able to extend or clarify their answers. This recapitulation can be planned into the schedule as an option at several points, to be used only if you judge they need it.

Notice how in these various tactics you are referring implicitly, sometimes explicitly, to the needs of this interview. They signal that it is not your arbitrary decision to intervene, you are doing it to ensure a successful interview on the lines that they have agreed with you. In this way the formal nature of the interview works in your favour.

You may be wondering: do you really have to 'go back to it later' as you promised? Will they remember if you don't? Will either of you remember the point you promised to go back to? An easy way out is to rely on your general sweeper question 'Is there anything else you want to say that I haven't covered?'

Sticky moments

Few people try to undermine your interview, but you may be faced with some awkward questions and situations.

- *'I really don't know that you should interview me.'*

    (This, after they have agreed to be interviewed, and you have included them in your sample on that understanding!) You can try to find out why they are now reluctant. They may be worried about confidentiality: you can repeat assurances in regard to this. If they feel they are not knowledgeable about the topic, you might say 'That's not uncommon, and I am keen to get a proper range of views from people like yourself. I don't just want the enthusiasts.' If they suggest you might try someone else, imply that you cannot really change your sample in the middle of things. Try to persuade them, as you may find that they have an interesting point of view to express.

- *'I'd rather you didn't record this.'*

    Again, you should have got prior agreement on this. Find out why they have changed their mind. Give further assurances on confidentiality, and emphasise that the tape is in the interests of accuracy, but be prepared to rely on notes if you have to.

- *'It's not convenient, I'm afraid. Could you come back later?'*

  If you can, do so. You should always take some other work with you when interviewing, just in case!

- *'Do you agree with that?'* or *'What do you think?'*

  The simplest answer is 'I can't say, not while I'm interviewing you'. (Don't tell them later either, because they may tell other people whom you still have to interview.)

- *'Who else have you been interviewing?'*

  'I can't say. Remember, the interviews are anonymous. I won't be able to tell anyone I have interviewed you, either.'

- *'What have people been saying?'*

  'I have only interviewed a few so far, there is no clear pattern yet.'

Very occasionally you may need to abort an interview, if you find that it is causing your respondent obvious distress, or if you are learning about criminal activities that you feel should not be kept confidential.

Piloting

Chapter 3 emphasises the need to plan your schedule carefully. Despite your preparation, you cannot know how the interview will work in practice, especially if you are interviewing various kinds of people. Piloting is essential.

In piloting you are trying to do two things: first, to give the interview a trial run under realistic conditions; second, to get as much information as possible from the other person about how they interpreted and reacted to your questions. You need to balance these conflicting requirements in choosing people and conducting the pilot interviews.

Choose interviewees for the pilot who are similar to the people in your study, ideally from the same 'population', but not individuals you intend to interview. Avoid members of your research team, or anyone who has been involved in preparing or shredding the schedule. They know too much to give it a realistic test. You need people who are sympathetic to the work, because you will be asking for a good deal of their time. They must also be likely to be forthright and incisive in their criticisms, trying to anticipate any difficulties or negative reactions that might arise with others. Inevitably you will find yourself calling on close colleagues, family and friends or their children, to represent the professionals, the public, or the pupils.

If you are dealing with someone in an unique position, such as the Chief Education Officer, the Director of a project, or the Principal of an institution, you cannot really pilot the interview. You could ask someone to role-play the part as a rehearsal. It also helps to leave this interview until late in the study, when you will be familiar with your schedule. In the unique case, you will not be so much concerned about comparability with other interviews. You can prepare specially, concentrating on stimulating a good, informative response.

Even if you do not plan to tape-record the other interviews, you should record the pilots. You can play the tapes more than once, and let others listen, to learn as much as possible. Videotaping is sometimes suggested, to look at non-verbal factors. This is worth considering but remember that people are likely to be affected by a camera's presence, and you may not get a 'true' pilot. Your main concern in the study in any case will be with the verbal record.

The first pilot interview

Your first pilot interview is likely to be the longest and most traumatic in the whole study! Be sure to time it. Go through it exactly according to the schedule. If the interviewee has difficulty at some point, mark this on the schedule but don't stop to discuss it. Immediately afterwards, ask for general reactions. Did they feel comfortable with the questions, did they have enough time to think about their answers? Did they feel they were being led, or under pressure to say more than they wanted to?

After a short break you should go over the questions, raising the points which you have noted, and inviting them to raise others. The de-briefing takes at least as long again as the interview itself. Ideally, you should play back the tape question by question to stimulate recall of how they were thinking and feeling at the time. Make careful notes of all comments, but do not feel obliged to incorporate all of them into a revised schedule, only those that you feel are likely to be of general significance across the range of interviewees. Avoid making the schedule longer and more complicated.

Revising and refining

It is quite common for the first pilot to throw up serious problems. An interview may take far longer than you expected, some questions may just not work, or you may be drawn into saying far more than you intended. Don't panic! Make any major changes to your schedule that you feel are necessary. You might discuss these with your pilot interviewee, and even try out some revised questions. Then pilot the revised schedule, with someone else. After this, and perhaps one further round of piloting, you should have a procedure that you know will work with most interviewees.

Having established the method from the interviewees' point of view, it is useful to run a few dummy interviews, without the de-briefing, to check it from your own point of view. This lets you test whether you can sustain a comparable pattern of questioning, prompting and probing across a series of interviews with different kinds of people; whether you can avoid leading, interrupting or talking too much; and generally, whether you are settling into a consistent technique for implementing your schedule. It suggests the range of answers you can expect, with any implications for the kind of analysis you had planned.

This second stage of piloting may lead to further refinement of technique, which could be important in preparing for a large-scale interview survey. In small-scale research, you may not afford the time. In that case, you can proceed with the real interviews and use the first few as second stage pilots, checking the usual aspects of technique.

As your research proceeds you will find that you know better what to expect. The interviews proceed more smoothly and probably tend to take less time. It is possible that you are developing bad habits! The increased fluency may come from your anticipating answers and subtly leading, prompting and closing off discussion. After every few interviews, listen to your most recent tape to check that your technique is not drifting away from what you intended.

Summary

This chapter has emphasised that:

- good preparation is more important than having 'interview skills'
- having a well-prepared schedule is vital: it helps achieve consistency across the range of interviews
- you should adopt a friendly but businesslike approach, to give the interviewee confidence in your ability to conduct a successful interview
- the formality of the interview can be used, for example, to encourage people to be explicit, and to cope with 'difficult' interviews
- there are various verbal and non-verbal tactics that allow you to exercise control without dominating or 'leading'
- you should keep checking your approach by listening to your tapes.

6

Analysing the Interviews

As a result of your interviews you will have a pile of tapes or detailed notes, representing the raw data from which you aim to extract the answers to your research questions. This involves three stages: *Data Preparation* in which you tidy up your raw data and put it into a form that is easy to work with; *Analysis*, in which you try various ways of categorising and reorganising the prepared data, seeking patterns in it that have a bearing on your research questions; *Summarising Results*, where you use the patterns to develop conclusions. This chapter looks at these in turn.

Data preparation

Time spent on careful data preparation will be amply repaid in the later stages. You are going to live with your data very closely for quite some time, working over each section repeatedly while trying to keep a sense of the whole. Well prepared data makes it easy become familiar with the full range of what you have collected while being able quickly to locate specific material.

Your main aim in data preparation should be to make the material manageable, while at the same time retaining as much of the original information as possible and avoiding any distortion. In the case of tape-recorded interviews an important question is whether to transcribe them verbatim. Some researchers regard this as essential, but they are usually working in the ethnographic tradition, in which it is important to have regard for the exact words that people use to express their ideas, and in which a study may be based on a small number of respondents interviewed in depth.

Advantages of transcription

One big advantage of transcription is that most people regard a transcript as providing a 'true' record of the original interview. Of course some information has been lost: the body language, facial expressions, tone of voice. But there is a safeguard against serious distortions such as the interviewer `leading' the respondents, reporting selectively or misrepresenting their answers. These would be obvious from a transcript.

A transcript can both enhance and demonstrate the soundness of your research. For example, you can give a copy to your interviewee to correct any errors of fact; you can ask someone else to check your analysis by repeating it on a sample of transcripts; you can easily extract quotations to highlight your conclusions, and you can appeal to the verbatim record if you are accused of misrepresenting anyone's views. (You could use the tape itself for some of these purposes but a paper copy is more convenient.)

There is an extra advantage if your transcript is made on a wordprocessor. Most wordprocessing packages nowadays have facilities for 'searching', 'cutting' and 'pasting' text, which is useful in analysis. There are also more specialised programmes designed specifically for analysing interview data and the like.

Disadvantages of transcription

The main problem with transcription is the amount of work and time involved. One hour of tape may mean:

- 2 – 3 hours work for a skilled audio typist
- twice that for a keyboard amateur
- twice that again if you are writing it yourself in longhand
- twice that again if it is a 'difficult' tape – such as a group interview, or a poor recording.

You may need as many days to transcribe the data as to collect it! You need also to consider the amount of material that will result: one minute of talk may produce a page of transcript. Obviously there are strong arguments for using transcription selectively. If you opt for transcription you should get help if you can. Bodies that support small-scale research may provide funds to employ a typist for an appropriate number of hours where transcription is essential. Even if you are doing the work yourself, it helps if you can borrow a proper transcription machine with a foot pedal control and headphones. This makes it easy to run the tape back over short sections to check details quickly.

Retaining information

In transcribing, some of the nuances of talk are lost, but a lot can be retained and represented in the text by comments or symbols. Keep this simple, and agree on a standard usage with everyone involved in transcribing and analysis the interviews. You might use ... for a pause, ...? for an 'interrogative' pause (usually the researcher prompting!), ?? for anything not clear on the tape. Comments may be marked by square brackets: [laughs] [both speak]. Because you are aiming to retain information and avoid distortion, the transcriber should not 'correct' language and grammar, and other utterances (er, mm? mhm and so on) should also be retained. Punctuation is a problem because it has no direct counterpart in speech. It is best kept to the minimum that can be inferred from the voice: ends of sentences and not much more.

The result of transcription can look strange at first, rather like hearing your voice on a recording for the first time. It may come as a shock to see how often you interrupt yourself, leave sentences unfinished and speak quite ungrammatically. This is a useful reminder of the nature of semi-structured interviewing. It is not just a matter of going out and collecting the answers to your research questions. The interview is a dialogue between two people, and its structure is shaped by the process of interaction: the interplay of question and answer, taking turns in speaking, both of you knowing what has already been discussed as you progress through a series of topics. The processes of analysis and interpretation involve dismantling this natural structure and reconstituting the material. This needs to be done in a disciplined way that can be explained and justified. Transcripts are working documents. They should allow plenty of space for annotation: double spaced text, wide margins, and pages ending at natural breaks in the interview. You may want to number the lines. Speakers can be identified by personal initials or by their roles (R = researcher, T7 = the seventh teacher interviewed).

It is useful to mark the point reached on the tape counter at the end of each paragraph or page, or any point where the tape is unclear. Tape counters are far from standard even on machines of the same make and if you want to be sure of locating a passage you may have to play it back on the machine on which it was transcribed. (Alternatively you can calibrate each machine by making a table or graph showing how counter settings correspond to the time elapsed from the start of a standard tape. This allows you to match settings on different machines.)

Partial transcription

Selective transcription reduces the time for the work itself and the time spent reading transcripts later. You may decide from the start to transcribe answers to certain questions only, or you may select passages for transcription as you go along.

Paste your interview schedule on to a large sheet of paper, allowing plenty of space to write in answers. Listen to the tape in short sections, filling in the straightforward answers as short notes based on the interviewee's own words. When you come to 'rich' material that merits transcription on a separate sheet, note the point on the tape counter, and deal with the passage later. At the same time make a note of any sections where you regard the material as irrelevant and decide not to include it in your record. You may want to review that decision later.

In this way you preserve a large proportion of the important information, with a significant economy of effort.

Summarising

A transcript comes close to being a 'true' record of an interview. Any distortion is likely to be incidental and random. Whenever you settle for making summary notes from a tape there is always a risk of more systematic distortion: through the process of selecting what is to be included and excluded, and the way in which you word your summary, you may unconsciously impart a personal bias.

You can apply various safeguards. One of the simplest is wherever possible to use only words and phrases used by the interviewee. A more formal procedure is to get a colleague to check for any subjective distortion on your part, by reading a sample of your summaries while listening to the tapes. A more powerful test is to ask your colleague to make an independent summary directly from the tape, using guidelines that you provide. If that is not feasible, you could do the repeat summary yourself after a break of a week or so. You can then compare the summaries and decide if discrepancies are significant, and you can also discuss whether the guidelines themselves are free of bias. If you are sharing the work as a team, this kind of procedure is essential in evolving guidelines that guarantee consistency.

Another possibility is to give some of your summaries and tapes back to the interviewees. In cases where you have not been able to tape-record the interview, this is the only method of checking. It can be tricky. Rather than commenting on the accuracy of your summary they are liable to want to expand or explain their answers, thereby introducing their own subjective bias into the interview record. You would obviously write up your notes and offer them for comment as soon as possible after the interview, while people are more likely to remember what they said, but even then it is doubtful whether their memory is more accurate than your note-taking, and it is difficult to prevent them revising what they said, to varying degrees, according to the individuals involved. This method is not very effective as an overall check on the reliability of your data preparation. However, it may pick up specific errors arising from inaccurate note-taking. This would imply giving every interviewee a chance to make corrections.

Data analysis

You now have a pile of transcripts or summary notes, and are ready to begin analysis aimed at finding answers to your research questions. Some interview questions on matters of straightforward information can be dealt with by simply coding and counting responses using methods similar to those used in questionnaires. This chapter is concerned with the more complicated questions, typical of semi-structured interviews: the kind that justify transcription or detailed notes. These answers need to be handled in the form of text. You will reorganise, categorise and summarise the text, to match your research questions. You may have to organise it differently for different questions, and all the time you need to keep track of where the material came from: which respondent, which interview question, produced this statement?

In all of this work it helps if you can work with a colleague. Sometimes you may want to 'brainstorm' together, at others you will work separately and then compare notes. For example, you might work together to generate ideas about the categories you will use in dividing up your material. You have to write down a working definition of each category, one that is valid (that is, it makes sense) in terms of your research. You can then try applying the categories to part of an interview and develop some 'ground rules' to resolve any difficulties in deciding what goes where. Finally, work separately applying the system of definitions and ground rules to three or four samples of material. If your analyses agree, then your system is reliable (that is able to be applied consistently). If necessary, modify the rules and repeat the reliability check, until you are both satisfied.

Tools of the trade

Researchers tend to develop their personal toolkit for analysing semi-structured interview data. This may include coloured pencils, text highlighters, scissors or a craft knife, glue or sticky tape, large sheets of paper and other devices for marking, separating and reassembling the text. Some examples of these techniques are given in the next section. You will evolve your own kit and methods to suit your approach and the circumstances in which you work. There are a few rules you should observe:

- Never work on your original transcript, only on a copy. Keep the original in transparent plastic pockets and make copies as you need them – you will need plenty!

- Mark all your transcripts with coloured stripes down the left hand margin, so that when you cut them up you can tell at a glance where each piece came from. You can develop a unique sequence for each page: with five colours and three stripes, you have 125 (=5^3) combinations.

- Before you begin your analysis, read over all the material at least once, to get a general feeling of what's there.

Nowadays there are special programmes for 'qualitative data analysis' running on personal computers. These are constantly improving, but at the time of writing, they are probably not helpful for small-scale researchers. To use them you need to have all your data in wordprocessed form in the first place. Also, some of the packages are difficult to learn, and they tend to create very large files which means that you need a fairly powerful machine with a large memory. These packages are valuable when large numbers of interviews have to be processed in a routine way, but you tend to lose the 'feel' of the data.

It is not worthwhile learning a package specially to use it in a one-off study with 20 interviews at most. However, if you are already an experienced wordprocessor you may be able to use the facilities in your usual package. For example you might develop simple 'macro' routines to gather all the answers to Question 10 into a single file, or to find all the occurrences of a key term, and print out the sentences in which it occurs.

Developing categories

The first task in data analysis is to gather together all the text that is relevant to each of your research questions. This is fairly straightforward if your interview questions are directly related to your research questions. For example, some years ago we asked teachers their views on four aspects of S1/S2 science: *integration of the sciences, mixed-ability teaching, teaching to objectives,* and *guided discovery.* For each aspect we wanted to know: did they approve of it, how did they put it into practice, did it achieve results? In planning the analysis we knew that teachers' views on the desirability of guided discovery were contained in the answers to questions 18, 18(a) and 18(b), and so for this part of the analysis we need only consider these and not the whole transcript.

Let's suppose that you are repeating this study, working from transcripts. First, the answers to these questions could be cut out and put in a pile – and so on for each research question in turn.

One snag is that people's answers may overlap across questions. Early answers may anticipate questions not yet asked, or interviewees may add further comments on an earlier topic. Should you shift the material to where you think it is relevant, or leave it exactly where they said it? This dilemma is a reminder of the very nature of semi-structured interviewing. Which structure is more important: the structure provided by your research questions, or by the interviewees' way of constructing their responses?

It may be best to compromise. Put a copy of the material where you think it belongs, dealing with it there, but marking where it came from ('from Q.6'). Leave a copy in its original position, marking where it will be dealt with ('see Q.2'). This reminds you that the interviewee saw a connection between these topics.

Categorising answers

The next task is to allocate the answers relevant to each research question into various sets of categories. In the case of questions about the desirability of guided discovery, some of the categories are fairly obvious: *answers in favour v. answers against* the method. Your interviewees probably answered your questions in the expectation that you would interpret the answers in this way.

Rather than cutting up the text further, you can mark it with highlighters: blue for favourable statements, red for unfavourable, with some text remaining unmarked. After trying this with two or three answers, you may find that some answers don't fit, and a third category is needed: conditional approval ('it would be OK if only we had more time/ better materials/ more able pupils'). Back to the drawing board, with a fresh text and *three* colours! Again you may find ambiguous statements: 'It would be OK if we had 2000 years to cover the syllabus.' Is this really 'conditional approval'? You need to make a decision, and develop a set of rules about what belongs in each category. Discuss these with your colleague, and then carry out a reliability check on their application.

Using established categories

Sometimes you may want to use an established set of categories derived from previous research by yourself or others. In our study we used a system based on one by Joseph Schwab (Schwab, 1962) for looking at the factors affecting curriculum innovations. This had six categories, relating to: *educational policy, resources, pupils' learning, effective teaching, the nature of the subject,* and *the expectations of society.*

To apply this you could use highlighters as before on a fresh text, or you could bracket lines of text with a marginal note to signify the category (Pol, Res, Pup, Tea, Sub or Soc). This is better when the categories may overlap.

Using a pre-determined general framework has some advantages. It avoids imposing your way of thinking. You can expect most of your material to fit in somewhere, but you may find that some categories remain empty, and this may be significant. We found that teachers said a great deal about learning and teaching, but next to nothing about the expectations of society. When we applied the same general framework in analysing the official curriculum guidelines, we found a very different emphasis.

Extracting categories from the data

The danger with predetermined categories is that you may distort the data to fit them. An alternative is to extract categories from the material itself. Select one of the fuller answers, and summarise it as a list of short points. Repeat this with one or two more answers, compare the lists, and try to make a composite list. Now summarise another answer and see whether it introduces anything not already on the list. Proceed in this way until you reach a stable, comprehensive list. Now try collecting the points into groups which have something in common. There may be several different ways of doing this, each of which may be useful.

For instance when teachers talk about guided discovery you may find a cluster of 'points' forming a theme of 'ways of giving guidance':

- providing work cards
- giving strict instructions at the start
- close supervision of activities
- checking and correcting their written notes.

Another theme might be 'purposes of guidance':

- ensuring safety
- making experiments work
- getting the right answer.

These two sets of categories probably overlap, and probably both would be useful. You want about six categories in any set, otherwise you are not simplifying the task of summarising. Some points may be mentioned only occasionally or seem quite separate, and you can put them in a 'miscellaneous' category. However, if you find this category becoming large, you should reconsider the items it contains.

Working from whole transcripts

If your interview questions are not directly related to particular research questions, you may have to work with whole transcripts. In a recent study of teachers' thinking, we based interviews on one general question: 'What went well in today's lesson?' with neutral probing on each item mentioned, to encourage people to talk at length. The analysis used a scheme derived from earlier research, with four categories relating to: *teachers' actions; pupil activity; pupil progress;* and *factors affecting the other three categories.* These were identified in the interviews as a whole, using four colours of highlighter on transcripts. (The four categories had been derived in a previous study using the method described earlier for extracting categories from the data. Again, this was applied to whole interviews rather than answers to specific questions.)

Summarising results

Surveying the whole sample

By reorganising the material you replace perhaps 20 unique answers with clusters of equivalent statements in each of a small number of categories. This allows you to summarise what people have said, and is the basis of the mini-survey approach. If you spread out your pile of answers on guided discovery you may see very little blue highlighting (showing outright approval), and roughly equal amounts of red (outright rejection) and yellow (conditional approval). How can you make this more precise? In semi-structured interview studies you should think carefully before using numbers or statistics. In this case it seems reasonable to suppose that people have taken sides, and so you may expect to count them up as pros or cons. However, if you look at the individual responses you may find that some are clearly positive or negative, but others give mixed responses. You need to make a judgement about each case, partly on the number of statements made in each category, but also considering their response as a whole. Your summary might be:

> 'Only 1 out of 19 gave outright support, while 9 out of 19 strongly rejected the method. 5 gave answers in which conditional acceptance predominated over rejection, while 4 expressed an even balance between these.'

Notice that actual numbers are quoted, as a reminder that the numbers are small. To claim that 47% rejected the approach (let alone 47.37%) would give the false impression of a large survey.

If you look at the result of applying Schwab's framework to the transcripts you may find that most statements are marked in the category of 'Resources' or 'Pupils' Learning', and that, curiously, nothing much is said in the 'Subject' category. You may also note that most of the 'Resources' statements are negative, and that the only positive comments refer to this being a good way for pupils to learn. How can this be presented?

In the previous example it was agreed that people would see the question as a chance to declare a position, and so each person could be counted. That does not apply in this case. You have not deliberately asked everyone about each of the six categories, and so you cannot assume that the things they have chosen to mention define each person's position totally. You cannot say that one interviewee is only and completely concerned about Resources as a reason for rejecting guided discovery, or that another is half concerned about Pupils' Learning and half about Policy constraints, because they mentioned both. In this case it is not reasonable to count people. But you might count the number of statements made in each of the categories, possibly presenting a table that cross-references your two sets of categories. The table highlights the existence of empty categories. Again, numbers of statements rather than percentages are quoted.

Statements About Guided Discovery

	Outright Rejection	Outright Acceptance	Conditional Acceptance
Resources	10	0	5
Policy	6	0	4
Learning	15	4	10
Teaching	6	0	3
Subject	1	0	0
Society	0	0	0

You may feel that counting statements rather than people will 'over-represent' the more talkative interviewees. However, you are not conducting a poll in which each person is entitled to an equal vote. It is an attempt to describe the variety and relative prevalence of views that a group of people hold and express when invited to do so.

Identifying group views
Your interviewees may fall into several groups. This may be part of your research plan. You may be doing comparative case studies of three schools, or you may have selected groups by 'quota sampling' (see chapter 4). On the other hand your sample may naturally contain people with different kinds of responsibilities or different levels of experience. Finally, 'groups' may emerge as you scan the data: you may become aware of people who seem to share a common point of view.

To identify groups, you can build group membership into your system of coding stripes. You can add an extra stripe at some stage, perhaps down the right hand margin. Lay out the responses and gather each group together on the table. You can now scan a group to see if there are noticeable characteristic patterns of highlighting or codings. Skim-read the responses to see if they are different from the overall picture. You might detect patterns such as the following:

- *some groups have more to say on certain issues:* promoted staff mention a wider range of factors than unpromoted
- *people talk about different things:* management teams talk about policy and cross-curricular issues, teachers talk about subject syllabuses and classroom management
- *people talk about the same things in different ways:* less experienced teachers talk about pupils in terms of behaviour and discipline, experienced teachers in terms of ability and learning
- *people talk about the same things in the same way, but disagree:* some departments are enthusiastic about change, others resist it.

In case studies and comparative case studies you will be particularly interested in the interrelationship within the groups forming each 'case'. You can look for similarities in what they talk about, how they talk about it, and the views they express, and also look for occasions when they express awareness of each others' perspectives and points of view.

The methods for exploring group views are exactly like those described already, applying extra caution because the groups are inevitably small and individuals are therefore significant. Before claiming that it is the group which has a distinctive view you might focus on various members and ask yourself: if this person had not been interviewed, would I still make the same claim about the group? or, would this person appear out of place in one of the other groups?

Individual perspectives

If you have gone through all the stages described so far, you should know your data pretty well! Much of the work involves chopping up the text and isolating items into categories. Nevertheless you should still have a strong sense of the individual interviewees and what they said to you. While there is interest in a survey across all the interviews, you may feel that there are also some important patterns in the ways in which individuals build up their accounts, emphasising certain factors, resisting particular ideas, arguing a consistent case as they see it, and giving evidence of a personal philosophy of educational practice.

To study an individual's perspective you need to reassemble the full interview, now probably in several versions with different sets of codings and comments. You can look for patterns in these, and also read the text as a whole looking for consistent and distinctive features:

- are particular factors mentioned repeatedly?
- are explicit connections made between different issues?
- is there a consistent perspective representing the 'management' view, a child-centred emphasis, or the 'culture' of a particular subject?
- is there a general tone: optimistic, conservative, disgruntled?

The aim is not, as a rule, to develop a detailed analysis of how each individual has made sense of the interview topic. (If that is your intention, then a fully ethnographic or life-history approach is more appropriate. These concentrate on understanding each individual's account in its own terms.) Rather, the exercise is useful as a counterpoise to a mini-survey approach, in which individual views are submerged in the description of the overall pattern. It can help you to avoid overestimating the degree of consensus, and you may want to provide a few illustrations of these different ways of thinking in your report.

Summary

This chapter has dealt with three processes.

Data Preparation should be done carefully. The aim is to make the material manageable without distorting it, and to retain the original information in the important areas. Selective transcription is highly desirable.

Analysis and *Summarising Results* – here a variety of approaches is possible, reflecting the flexibility of the semi-structured interview:

- The original structure of the interview can be dismantled and replaced by one based on the research questions; later, the original structure may be re-created to gain a different insight.
- The categories for analysis might be obvious from the interview questions, or categories used in other similar research, or categories extracted from the interview data.
- The summary patterns could involve the whole sample, or groups, or individuals.
- The judgements made may be quantified, or remain purely qualitative.

BUT

- The process must always be clearly thought out and all procedures made explicit and checked by colleagues.

7

Reporting and Communication

The final stage in your research is to decide what you have learned, and what you want to tell others. The two are closely connected. People do not usually get involved in educational research purely to satisfy their own curiosity, they do it in the hope of improving education, and that involves communicating with others. You may have had these others in mind from the start: people in similar circumstances to yourself, people like those you have been interviewing, people with responsibility for the area you have investigated.

Educational research does not give us foolproof recipes that tell us what to do. Its findings take the form of better information and understanding, of ideas that help us to make sense of what is going on, to understand the factors that are important and how they influence events, or to decide on the criteria by which we can evaluate our practices. The researcher's job is not complete until these ideas have been passed on. Others have to work out the implications for their own circumstances, and use your ideas to guide their decisions and activities.

It helps to think of reporting as teaching others what you have learned, the hard way, by doing research. It is often said that we never really understand something until we have to teach it. As you prepare to communicate your findings, you are forced to reflect critically and question the significance of each in turn: how do I know this? am I sure? and above all: does it matter? Why does anyone need to know this? Before you can convince others you have to convince yourself, and if you cannot answer these questions confidently, think again. The hardest aspect of reporting is to recognise that the value of a particular finding bears no relation to the effort it cost you, and discard it.

Reporting has several purposes which ideally should involve three stages:

- letting others scrutinise the work to establish its soundness
- sharing the new understanding you have gained
- considering the implications for practice and policy.

You should aim to complete each in turn though in practice you cannot usually treat them as separate exercises.

Planning an oral report

In academic circles research is traditionally reported through a formal written account such as a thesis, a journal article or a report to a commissioning body. However this chapter concentrates on oral reporting, partly because this is strongly preferred within the teaching profession, but mainly because the discipline of preparing a talk to colleagues helps you to think of reporting as an exercise in communication, and so, to keep your message clear and uncluttered. Much of the advice that follows is equally relevant to the planning of a written report, which is discussed later.

Let's suppose you have the opportunity to talk about your research at a conference or in-service event, at a staff meeting or to a group of teacher researchers. This does not mean literally 'reading a paper' to a passive audience. Interaction and discussion are encouraged and if you are offered half an hour for your presentation you are probably expected to leave 10 minutes for questions. (If you don't, people will suspect that you are trying to run away from any critical discussion!) It certainly will not do to wait until the last minute and then compile some extracts or a digest from a lengthy written report.

Even if you have to prepare a text which may be published as part of the conference proceedings you also need a working script for your talk. Text and script work in different ways. When people read your text it is all available to them and they can scan backwards and forwards and build up their understanding in their own way and in their own time. When you speak from your script you control their pace of learning and so you have to do a lot of the work for them. You can think of it as a traditional lesson in which you are teaching your audience what you learned, and use all the traditional teaching skills: creating a simple structure, emphasising a few key points, reinforcing these through examples and repetition, and integrating each in turn into people's overall understanding of the topic.

The first section of the talk should aim at establishing confidence in your work.

Introduction

In teaching you try to start by establishing what people know already. However, you can hardly ask a large audience of fellow professionals questions round the class! It is likely that your research will have given you some idea of the range of knowledge and opinions that you will find among colleagues. You can use this, and introduce your research in a way that will feel familiar and give the audience confidence. As you outline the area and the problem you also give them the necessary few minutes to 'tune in' to the tone of your voice and the pace and style of your presentation before you present them with any challenging new ideas that they need to wrestle with.

By the end of your introduction you should have prepared them for the transition from their *practitioner's perspective* on the topic to your *researcher's perspective*. A good way to effect this change and set up the framework for what follows is to end with a transparency showing your main research questions.

Methodology

It is useful to give a brief account of your methodology at this stage. This again is in order to create confidence: confidence in yourself as someone who knew what they were doing and did it thoroughly; confidence in your findings as having a systematic and rigorous basis, and therefore not to be equated with impression and anecdote. You need to establish the boundaries of that confidence, making clear the areas in which you will speak on the basis of your research and others where you do not claim that sort of authority.

This helps to convince your audience to take your ideas seriously and more generally it helps educate them to understand what research can and cannot offer them. However, it does not count as an occasion for validating your research and you should avoid being drawn into extended discussion of issues in methodology. (If some people are keen to discuss these you can agree to talk about it later.) Above all, do not give them a detailed account of all your activities and decisions. It may have been agony and ecstasy for you, but they really don't need to know!

What you *do* need is a short non-technical statement covering three main points in particular: *the sampling, the interviewing, and the analysis.*

The sample

Your choice of people to interview is important because it limits the claims that you will make. For example, if your research is a case study of one school then the findings refer to the special conditions in that school. Draw attention to particular circumstances that are reflected in the findings and say how far you believe they are typical. Or, if you carried out a small-scale survey, define the population precisely and if sampling was involved make it clear that this was done systematically (it is better not to say 'randomly'!).

The interview

Researchers would understand what you mean by 'semi structured interviews using no prompts and only neutral probes', but with fellow professionals you should provide an example: possibly a transparency showing one main question and the immediate follow-up, thus allowing you to explain the style of questioning and the different purposes of prompting and probing.

Analysis

The analysis can be dealt with similarly by showing a section of a transcript with coloured underlinings or a collection of statements gathered under one heading, in order to illustrate the process of analysis. You should mention the ways in which you checked your analysis with colleagues or the interviewees themselves.

Presenting the findings

The next stage is to present your findings. There is a temptation to get bogged down in details and to work your way laboriously through each interview question in turn presenting tables of results or lists of quotations covering all the different answers that you were given. That is not what you should be doing. The audience does not need an exhaustive description of your data. At this point they should have accepted that what you will tell them is soundly based on the interview evidence. Now they want to hear what you have learned!

The importance has been emphasised of organising an oral presentation around a few key points. An obvious framework is provided by your research questions. You might structure the presentation of your findings by preparing a series of transparencies each of which carries one of your research questions and three or four bullet points offering the answers. You can talk around this material but keep going back to emphasise the 'bullets'.

Points about wording

You can do a lot to prevent misunderstanding of your report if you pay attention to key points of wording.

Take account of what they know

As you 'teach' people what you have learned you need to consider how this new understanding relates to what they know already, from experience and common sense, and present your arguments accordingly. If the research confirms what they believed anyway then their reaction may be 'who needs it?'. You need to stress what the research adds to our intuitive knowledge: you can provide the evidence to support what individuals suspected, and that will be important in arguing for change. You may be able to demonstrate how ideas apply in a range of circumstances, draw attention to exceptions and possibly explain *why* things are as they are.

If the research contradicts what people believe their reaction may be to reject it outright. You can stress that you began by 'knowing' what they know. If you now think differently it's not because you are any smarter than they are but because the weight of evidence from your research forced you to think differently. You can then invite them to follow you through that learning process.

Distinguish facts from findings

Politicians are fond of saying 'the fact of the matter is ...' and then launching into a lengthy statement which is not at all a matter of fact but an opinion, that they would like you to accept. A researcher must distinguish between fact and opinion! From your research you have a body of 'facts': the 'facts' of what people said to you in interviews. They may have said (for example) that:

> 'the new policy is rubbish'
>
> 'everyone says the new policy is rubbish'
>
> 'we aren't following that new policy'
>
> 'we can't follow the new policy here'
>
> 'the new policy isn't working'
>
> 'the new policy wouldn't work here'.

They may have gone on to offer reasons and quote evidence in support of these statements. On the basis of these 'facts', you can report as 'findings': people's personal opinions, people's judgements of what is feasible, people's accounts of their own activities, people's criteria and evidence for making judgements, and some account of people's reasoning.

But, you cannot report as 'findings': whether the new policy is any good, what people actually do, or whether the new policy is working, let alone whether the new policy can work. To distinguish facts from findings you may make frequent use of phrases such as:

> 'in the interviews people said that ...'
>
> 'when asked (this question) people expressed the view ...'
>
> 'the main reason that people offered was ...'

Setting limits to your claims

If as suggested you have set out the details of your sample and the range of your research questions, then you can be quite firm about the limits of what you know and refuse to be drawn beyond that. It helps to use phrases such as:

'the headteachers interviewed in this study ...'

'in each of these three schools ...'

'for this sample of 5 year olds ...'

You can resist attempts to have you extrapolate and speculate about other circumstances and rebut attempts to attack the research based on isolated examples ('.. not in my school it wouldn't!'). You might plan a standard response to such kinds of questions:

'This is a case study of a particular school in which these factors have emerged as significant. If your circumstances are substantially different then it is possible that a similar study would highlight different factors.' (Making the point that no 'similar study' has yet been done.)

'A sample, however systematically selected, cannot cover all possibilities. I can only say that amongst 20 teachers I interviewed, no-one offered the view that you mention.' (Again stressing that you have the evidence to support what you say, whereas they do not.)

Avoid taking sides

Educational debate is often polarised and people may press you to take sides and say which view is 'right'. In reporting you should aim at proportional representation and you need to be particularly careful about quoting numbers (a point that has already been made in chapters 4 and 6). For example, if you ask 20 people the same question and 11 express one view and 9 another, you do not have a clear majority, but a fairly even split between two commonly held views. When people have not been asked directly but express a view spontaneously then even smaller numbers may be significant. Six out of 20 cannot be dismissed as 'a minority' since you do not know that the others reject this view or regard it as unimportant.

Be precise. State clearly whether your evidence supports a conclusion, or suggests alternatives, or is divided, or is insufficient, or is inconclusive, or rejects a view but does not offer an alternative.

Some points on presentation

Oral presentations at conferences are often not well done, even by professional researchers. A common tendency is to swamp the audience with details and overrun the time available. This may be because people are extremely enthusiastic about all that they have done, or it may be a sign of insecurity. It is easy enough to avoid this if you prepare properly, remembering that what you need is a script rather than a text. If you make a list of your main points and then talk aloud about each in turn you can develop a draft script based on how you naturally express your ideas in speech. Try to keep to standard spoken English as much as possible, avoiding the in-house jargon of both the research profession and the teaching profession. Where precise terminology is necessary you can insert a brief 'gloss' in the script as each term is introduced.

A typed script with the lines double spaced will have about 200 words on a page. Since formal presentation operates at half the speed of ordinary conversation this will take about two minutes to deliver. This pace will allow you to maintain intermittent eye contact with your audience while you read from the script (especially if you use a lectern: if necessary, improvise one!) Rehearse your talk allowing time for any use of an overhead projector or other visual aid. If it takes too long, cut it! – don't rely on speeding up your delivery – and plan also to make a further cut if, as often happens, you find that your session is late in starting.

It is fairly common for presenters not to prepare a script, but to rely on a series of overhead transparencies talking about each in turn. This can result in excessive use of the projector and has become known as 'death by 1000 transparencies'. I much prefer using the projector sparingly to provide some variety of stimulus and to pin down key points. One transparency showing your research questions, one or two used in passing to illustrate the interviewing technique, and one for each main research question setting out the findings, is plenty. (This last set is often very useful when dealing with questions.)

The projector is invaluable if you use it well. Do not cram too much material on the screen and allow the audience enough time to digest it. I now use large type, say 20 or 24 point, both to ensure legibility and to reduce the amount of information I display. It is worth remembering that people can read text on the screen two or three times faster than you can speak it aloud so the best approach is often to announce what you're going to show them, display it, and then step aside, allowing them to digest the information without the distraction of your voice.

It is quite different with transparencies showing tables of data or diagrams representing conceptual relationships. People need help and a good deal of time to grasp what these are about. If used they should be kept as simple as possible.

Considering implications

Once you have presented your findings you can invite questions aimed at clarifying and consolidating people's understanding of your research. Until this process is complete you should try to postpone discussion of questions about the implications of the work for policy and practice. This is partly because when you do make the transition to discussing implications, there is a significant shift in your relationship with your audience. When discussing your research you are 'the authority' and they are learning from you. But when discussing implications, they become the ones with special knowledge, about their own circumstances and the scope for action that these circumstances allow. Your research cannot offer them a prescription guaranteed to work in that unique context, even if they expect it of you.

For that reason it is good if you can mark the transition by changing the format of the interaction, for example by moving into small groups to tackle an agenda that you may have suggested, or even by reassembling on another occasion after people have prepared their own agenda to which you can then respond. (These possibilities are particularly suited to in-service work.)

In your new role you might have two main purposes:

• first, to continue to develop people's understanding of your findings and caution them against over or under estimation of their relevance to their own context.

- second, to prompt them towards a more explicit understanding of their own circumstances. What factors are important in their schools? What range of action is feasible? How do they know? Or how could they find out? And how would they evaluate the effectiveness of any action taken?

In this way you are not only disseminating your findings with a proper respect for the knowledge of your fellow professionals, but also encouraging them to ask research questions themselves.

Writing for the professional audience

Teachers like to meet the researcher in person and ask questions. They are reluctant to read research reports, possible because they have been put off by the style of articles in learned journals. Yet written reports are important: they are more permanent, more detailed and more precise than word of mouth. One reason for considering oral reporting first in this chapter is my feeling that a well prepared talk, along the lines indicated, is an excellent basis for a written account aimed at a professional audience. The discipline of treating reporting as a process of teaching and learning, of stripping down the account to its essentials, structuring it around the research questions, providing detail only selectively, and taking care over key points in wording, provides a robust framework. If this is retained in the written version, you can easily add a more detailed account of the data and expand the explanation of complex issues. The main structure of the argument remains clear, the style stays 'friendly' and people can cope with the extra detail because they are now working at their own pace as they read it.

Using quotations

One aspect of the written report that deserves some attention is the use of quotations. When reporting research you want to remind people that what you say is based on evidence, and that the connections and conclusions you make stem from significant patterns in the data. With a large questionnaire study you can do this by means of numbers, presenting tables and graphs, and quoting tests of statistical significance. In a small interview study, other means must be found. Quotations remind people of your evidence, and are especially useful if they show that interviewees themselves make the same connections and share your interpretations.

But don't overdo it. In ethnography, where the aim is to 'see the world through others' eyes' it is reasonable for the text to consist largely of quotations, with the researcher's words providing a commentary. However, your report should emphasise *your* research questions and the answers to them, with quotations serving merely to illustrate. Most of the results can be reported in indirect speech, with one or two quotations added per page. These should be chosen carefully.

- *Very brief quotations are not effective.* Occasionally, verbatim phrases can be 'highlighted' in the body of the text, but the main quotations that are marked by indentation should be a few lines long.

- *They should be unambiguous.* Each should clearly support the point you are making and representing a firmly held view of the speaker.

- *They should add something to the text.* They may extend the meaning in terms of individual circumstances, which you could not do in making the general point, or express it is a lively and individual way. The readers should sense a different voice that speaks to them directly.

- *They should reflect the broad balance of the data.* If you look at all your quotations together, the majority should deal with common or important points; they should represent the balance of positive and negative views; and several different interviewees should be represented.

Even if people have told you that they won't mind being quoted, they may change their minds when they see something in print. Ensure that anyone being quoted cannot be identified from the report. Where this is not possible, check their agreement specifically by showing them the draft report.

Summary

This chapter has identified three purposes in dissemination and the different roles and methods of communication that the researcher may need to adopt:

- *validation,* that is, presenting an account of the methods used to allow people to judge their soundness
- *presenting findings:* that is, sharing the new understanding gained from the research with members of the profession
- *considering implications,* with the researcher acting as a consultant to peer groups of fellow practitioners.

In presenting findings you may start with an oral presentation that can be developed into a fuller written report. It helps if you:

- think of it as a piece of traditional teaching
- structure it clearly around your research questions
- avoid getting bogged down in detail
- be clear about what you can claim, and don't be drawn into speculation.

Chapter 1 pointed out that interviewing is popular because, in the teaching profession, 'the natural thing to do is to talk to people', and so it seems appropriate that this final chapter should emphasise oral presentation and the use of quotations to add credibility. Yet the reliance on the spoken word is not necessarily a strength. Talk is, relatively, impermanent, imprecise and unreliable. An interview study does more than gather talk, sort it out and pass it on. You are not simply helping the profession to talk to one another. You are distilling out a better kind of understanding than the talk itself expressed: in today's phrase, 'adding value'.

This better understanding may suggest improvements in the immediate area that you have studied. If you write up your research – but only if you write it up – then others can test your ideas and so gain improved insight into their own areas. In this way your small-scale study can contribute to a more general build-up of understanding, and to the cumulative influence on practice and policy that we hope for from research of all kinds.

Further Reading

If you wish to pursue your interest in interviewing, then you should find useful texts in your local college or university library. Under 'Interviewing' you can pick out titles that deal specifically with interviewing in research. In the sections on education, sociology, and social sciences generally, you will find books about research methods in general which may contain good chapters on interviewing and other techniques, with helpful follow-up references.

One text dealing with a variety of interviewing methods is:

Powney, J & **Watts, M** (1987) *Interviewing in Educational Research.* Routledge.

A book which also includes other techniques:

Oppenheim, A N (1993) *Questionnaire Design, Interviewing and Attitude Measurement.* Pinter. This tends to emphasise unstructured and highly structured methods, rather than semi-structured, but has plenty of good advice to offer.

Useful chapters on interviewing can be found in:

Cohen, L & **Manion, L** (1994, 4th edition) *Research Methods in Education.* Routledge.

Bell, Judith (1987) *Doing Your Research Project: a guide for first time researchers in education and social science.* Open University Press.

Kane, E (1990) *Doing Your Own Research: how to do basic descriptive research in the social sciences and humanities.* M. Boyars.

Finally for a text with exercises, you could look at the materials produced for the Open University course:

DEH 313 *Principles of Social and Educational Research* (1993), or even its predecessor E341 *Methods of Educational Enquiry,* dating from 1973.

References

Brown, S & McIntyre, D (1993) *Making Sense of Teaching.* Open University Press. See Chapter 3 in particular.

Lewis, I & Munn, P (1987) *So You Want to Do Research! A guide for teachers on how to formulate research questions.* SCRE Practitioner Minipaper 2.

Schwab, J J (1962) The teaching of science as inquiry. In: Schwab, J J & Brandwein, P F (eds) *The Teaching of Science.* Harvard University Press.

THE SCRE 'USING RESEARCH' GUIDES

Lewis, Ian & **Munn, Pamela** (1987) *So You Want to Do Research! A guide for teachers on how to formulate research questions.* Practitioner Minipaper 2.

Munn, Pamela & **Drever, Eric** (1990) Revised edition 1995. *Using Questionnaires in Small-Scale Research: a teacher's guide.* Practitioner Minipaper 6.

Drever, Eric (1995) *Using Semi-Structured Interviews in Small-Scale Research: a teacher's guide.* Practitioner Minipaper 15.

Simpson, Mary & **Tuson, Jennifer** (1995) *Using Observations in Small-Scale Research: a beginner's guide.* Practitioner Minipaper 16.

Suggestions for further titles are welcome.